A BIRMINGHAM BACKSTREET BOYHOOD

GRAHAM V. TWIST

ISIS
LARGE PRINT
Oxford

First published in Great Britain 2008
by
The History Press

Published in Large Print 2010 by ISIS Publishing Ltd.,
7 Centremead, Osney Mead, Oxford OX2 0ES
by arrangement with
The History Press

British Library Cataloguing in Publication Data
Twist, Graham V.
    A Birmingham backstreet boyhood. - -
(Reminiscence)
    1. Twist, Graham V. - - Childhood and youth.
    2. Poor - - England - - Birmingham - - Biography.
    3. Birmingham (England) - - History - - 20th
century.
    4. Birmingham (England) - - Social life and
customs - - 20th century.
    5. Large type books.
    I. Title II. Series
    942.4'96084'092–dc22

ISBN 978–0–7531–9580–2 (hb)
ISBN 978–0–7531–9581–9 (pb)

Printed and bound in Great Britain by
T. J. International Ltd., Padstow, Cornwall

Contents

Dedication

This book is dedicated to my family, both present and past, and to the people of Nechells and Aston during my childhood — most of them who have long since passed away. These people, who are still alive in my head, visit me in one way or another most days; a smell here or a word there is enough to trigger-off some old memory. I only have to see a blue-and-white hand-made glass swan and my sweat-stained dad working in front of a red-hot glass-blowing furnace appears before my eyes; a certain type of laugh and my mom is by my side. The same thing happens with my brother Terry and my sister Von; I see a Scout and there is Terry, resplendent in his uniform; I hear a chattering excited voice and it's my sister Von. Both have now passed away but still remain within my heart. A walk up the Lickeys and I am transported back sixty years to what seemed like mile-long queues up Hill Street, the bone-rattling tram ride from Navigation Street along the Bristol road through the conker trees, drinking cold tea out of a milk bottle, and eating lard sarnies covered in salt and pepper and seeing the men standing in clusters drinking their pints outside the Hare and Hounds.

These memories are now but burnt into my very being because that's what families are. We are all individuals but we are all part of the whole. My family, neighbours, friends, teachers and everyone I met during my childhood shaped me and thousands like me as if we were painted onto a canvas. We are there for all the world to see, warts-and-all and nothing will ever alter us. And being Brummies and working-class, we should be proud of what we are.

A special mention needs to be made about my mate Alec Moss. We spent our formative years together as mates, and at seventeen would have died for each other. We worked together, courted together, went away together, fought and drank together. Sadly, Alec passed away last year, but I know he and his wife Josie and their children were as close as could be. He was a loving man and it showed.

So to the people of Nechells, Aston and Brum, Cromwell Street School, Cowper Street School and Summer Lane School, I thank you; you played a part in making me what I am and for that I am eternally grateful. I know that any one of you could have written this book.

Foreword

by Professor Carl Chinn MBE

Our Mom comes out of Whitehouse Street, Aston. Her address was 7 back of 6. "Back of": it is a term that puzzles and baffles those who have no understanding of how the working-class of Birmingham lived — but for those, many whose address was also "back of", then it is a phrase that is infused with pronounced senses of identity, belonging, loyalty and sharing. Our Mom's house is long gone. There is a peck, an open space, where it stood with others that were "back of", but she sees it yet in her mind. You came down Whitehouse Street from the Aston Road North, past the Albion pub that is still on the corner, and then there were two houses, an entry, and two more houses. The house on the right of the entry was number 6. Up the entry was a yard. They were called "courts" officially and this one was Court 2, Whitehouse Street, but to Our Mom and her pals it was simply, yet powerfully, "our yard", and there were hundreds upon hundreds of other "our yards" in working-class Brum. In that yard there were four houses that backed on to the four that fronted the street. At a right angle, opposite the last of these, was a terrace of eight blind backs. They had no houses sharing their back wall as did a true back-to-back, but like them, they had no windows at the rear, for their back wall was also the wall of the playground of St Mary's Infants School.

That yard had two shared brew'ouses in which the mothers did the washing in a copper on the day allotted to them. It had the miskins, a walled-off area where the dustbins were kept, and six lavatories shared between two or three families. As Our Mom says, there was nothing romantic in living in a back house with one small room downstairs which served as living room, dining room, kitchen, drying room and much else besides. There was nothing romantic in sleeping in a small attic above the one bedroom and having to burn the bugs off the ceiling with a candle before you got into bed. That was because even though Our Nan was spotless, the houses were badly built with dirt instead of sand for the mortar, and horses' hair had been used to bind the plaster. There was nothing romantic about going to the lavatory down the yard in the dark, wet and wind and with a candle guttering in a jam jar, hoping the light would not go out.

Hardships and bad housing are not romantic, but for all that Our Mom is proud to be a backstreet Brummie whose address was "back of". She is proud of her Granny Wood who laid out the street's dead and brought babbies into the world, not charging any money but doing so because that was her role. She is proud of how her Mom and Dad collared all the hours that God sent and strove for a better life, and of how they gave her the values of respect, determination, doggedness, perseverance, cleanliness, patriotism, sharing what little you had, giving more than taking, and kinship. She is proud of her neighbours who clung fast to the same values, despite the poverty, rows and pollution. She is proud that her street was tough but safe for children, women and old people. And I know she will be proud of Graham Twist's compelling account of his younger life because it is a testament to all those whose address was "back of".

Graham was also a backstreet kid and is rightly proud to have been so. This story is his own, but I see in it Our Mom's story and the untold stories of all those hundreds of thousands of other Brummies who were also backstreet kids. He shirks not from the hard times — the overcrowding, the coats on the bed, the bucket in the bedroom, the free school meals, the picking up of the dog-ends off the street so that his Dad could make up a fag, the maiming of his Mom at work, the bare floorboards, the fights, and the shattered dreams. He movingly recounts the suicide of his Dad, a hard-working man whose pride and soul were broken by a society that cared nothing for working men when they could not work. But Graham also brings to life the high days, the holidays and the happy days — the horses trimmed up for May Day, the VE Day Party, the camping trip to Bewdley, going to the flicks on a Saturday morning, expeditions to Perry Barr Park, cycling to the country, games in the yard and the street, having a mooch on the monkey run, and so much more. Graham is a talented storyteller. He is the storyteller of his family and he is the storyteller of all backstreet Brummies. That is his gift and his talent. They are precious things. His Mom and Dad would be proud that one of theirs tells so well not only their story but also the story of so many.

CHAPTER
ONE

A Family Life

In 1945, when I was about four, on a damp and foggy day, I jumped off the wall at the bottom of our yard in Charles Arthur Street, Nechells Green. Me and my mates were playing at cowboys and Indians — and in our imaginations the wall was a rock face. We were jumping off this wall onto the miskins, which back in those days only really contained ash from the fires. Unfortunately, my mate at the time, John, thought it would be a good idea to take off the lid as I was in full flight. The results of which I have carried with me ever since in the shape of a broken, flattened nose. As my mother recalled it, she heard a piercing scream from one of my sisters and on coming out of our two-up one-down terraced house, was confronted with the sight of her youngest son covered from head to toe in grey and white ash, and with red, blue and green snot and blood pouring down his face.

Our terraced house at 5 Poplar Terrace was like thousands of other houses in Brum at that time; one room downstairs and two upstairs. The two-up wasn't quite accurate because the little room was absolutely minute. My eldest brother and our Uncle George slept in this small room, which had a single bed in it. The big room had two three-quarter sized beds in it; in one slept our mom and my other brother during the night, and our dad during the day. Dad was on permanent nights at a glass-blowing company in Phillips Street, Aston. In the other bed I slept between my two elder sisters. The beds all had old coats on them as well as blankets, but sheets were an unheard of luxury we could never afford. Because he slept during the day, we had to make sure we didn't wake our dad up. For six days a week my dad was just a lump in a bed; he used to sleep with his head under the blankets, to keep out the cold and the noise of his five kids. Obviously with three in a bed, space was at a premium, and I found that if I lifted myself up slightly, the gap I left would soon be taken over. This sometimes led to pushing wars with one of my sisters pushing with her feet on the wall and the other pushing back with her feet on the fire grate.

Domestic electricity was not available to us then and these rooms were supposed to be lit by gas mantles, though we never seemed to be able to afford them. The results of not using gas mantles were big, black soot marks on the ceilings. The distempered walls were home to a myriad of small creatures, fleas and the like, but the worst one of all was the bed bug. These things used to creep out of the cracks in the plaster at night, get into the bed and feed on your body while you were asleep, sucking on your blood like miniature vampire bats, and when they were full they used to look like fat red match heads. If you flattened them, the blood used to squirt all over the place. Our bedroom wall was full of little red shell-bursts of blood. I must have copied something I had seen at the pictures, because I once set fire to our bed by making a funeral pyre of matches. When our mom found out she gave me a right whaling, and I was never allowed near matches again.

During the night there was a bucket on the corner of the stairs for anyone who got caught short. Walking through the dark yard in the middle of winter on a cold, wet and windy night for a pee was not advisable. There was supposed to be a rota for emptying this galvanised receptacle in the toilet down the yard, but being the youngest, I had my fair share of struggling with this smelly thing, and as you came downstairs when you got up, it was best to try to avoid it. One day one of my sisters actually had the misfortune of falling head first into it.

When you got to the bottom of the stairs, in front of you was the large, chipped crock sink with its single brass cold water tap. We also had a black gas stove in the kitchen. You then turned right into what was called the living room. This room contained a black leaded grate for cooking rabbit stews in the hanging pot, drying the washing, and heating. We all had a turn at black leading this grate, and whoever did it had to work really hard to get it up to any sort of standard that would suit our mom.

In the winter everyone sat huddled around this tiny fire and most of us had red and blue mottled legs from standing too near to it. Your face and front used to be red hot and your back would be freezing, but the sight of those flames flickering away in all colours could take you off day-dreaming to another world. We would do toast against the little grill in front of the fire and there was always a black kettle, which was our teapot, hanging from the hook above the flames. Because they were coal fires, the chimneys used to catch fire quite regularly, and if you called the fire brigade out they would generally wait around till it burned itself out. We had to call out the brigade once and it made me feel so important to have these big men with their shiny hats and axes in our house. I think you had to pay for these call-outs, so people thought very carefully before sending for the fire brigade. When the chimney sweep came, he used to cover the front of the grate with sacking and push his brushes up and down the chimney. He'd then get you to go outside to see if you could see his brush. Because everyone had a coal fire, the fogs we would get were really thick — so thick that sounds would be muffled, and sometimes you would not be able to see a yard in front of you. It was strange to walk around in these pea-soupers, arms outstretched, with ghostly figures appearing out of the gloom, and the beacons of the street gas lamps shining like weak suns in a mist. Motor vehicles were a rarity so that walking in the horse road was no problem during these foggy attacks.

Saturdays used to be a mixture of high excitement equally balanced by periods of pure boredom. The high excitement came from going to the pictures up on Aston Cross. The boredom came from having to listen to the radio; because we had no electricity, this radio was powered by acid-filled accumulators which were obtained from a shop on Nechells Green. We took it in turns to take and fetch these accumulators, which, if you shook them too much, could splatter battery acid over you. This had a two-fold effect; one was that it burned through whatever you were wearing, and the other was that it burned your skin underneath. On a Saturday afternoon the radio would report live on a local football match. Our mom used to give me and our Von, my sister, a tanner each, four pence for the pictures, a halfpenny each for the number eight bus there and back and a penny for some kali. We usually walked there and back to save a penny to spend on some other little goodies. As you went past the Hen and Chickens pub, and opposite the Tubes, there was a little car park with small concrete stumps along the front of it. One Saturday I leap-frogged over one of them and our Von followed suit; unfortunately she was wearing a skirt which caught on the stump and threw her head first onto the gravel. She cut the underside of her chin and was scarred for life.

We still went to the flicks and she made me promise on pain of death not to tell mom how it had happened.

When you got to Aston Cross you had a choice; you could go left to the Astoria, or right to the Aston Cross picture house. The vinegary smell of the Ansells brewery was always in your nostrils and pervaded the whole area with a rich smell of hops and beer. Whichever pictures you went to, the fare seemed to be the same, with long boring court scenes of the captured Germans being sentenced, and fat old men telling us how they would change the world. But then came the highlight of the week — the serials. Who can recall the excitement of Flash Gordon versus Ming, Tarzan fighting the crocs and lions? It was a wonder there were any animals left in Africa the way he used to go through them! I can still remember Roy Rogers, a clean-cut cowboy and his little hairy mate, Gabby Hayes, riding off singing into the sunset.

The Aston Road was full of kids, like flocks of sparrows, all riding their imaginary trusty steeds to all points of the compass. You had to hold your left hand in front of you, as if you were holding the reins and with your right hand you slapped your arse and ran as fast as you could, clicking your tongue to sound like horses' hooves, and none of the Redskins could ever catch you. Or would you be Flash Gordon escaping from the evil clutches of Ming the Merciless at the beginning of the picture, and ending with him in an impossible life-threatening situation? Come back next week and see how he gets away. At the end of the picture, the National Anthem was played and everyone stood and clapped.

After riding your horse home, kicking the dog shit puff balls on the way, the boredom began. On the radio was live commentary of some football game or other — nothing to do, nowhere to go. The only excitement for us kids was sitting listening to the football results and trying to guess the scores before they were announced. The one good thing about Saturdays was that it was our dad's only day off work. He used to spend his daytime in the Beehive pub on Nechells Green. If he wasn't in bed for the afternoon, he used to play acrobats and balancing games with chairs; anything to keep us amused. Because he was a glass-blower, our dad had no "swallow", and consequently could down a pint in seconds. This ability brought him many a free pint when matched against other fast drinkers, but I never saw him out of order or aggressive as a result of it. Our dad was all of five foot tall and was known to one and all as Titch. He was partially blind and had a hole in his head I could get my little finger into. He had lost all his teeth, but could still eat an apple with his bare gums. These scars were the result of him getting hit by a number eight bus early one morning while walking home from work in the blackout during the war. They thought he was dead and threw a sack over him so that people wouldn't see his injuries.

Once our mom bought me a second-hand pilot's leather helmet. It was miles too big for me, but I wore it day and night nevertheless. One day running up the street it fell over my eyes and I ran into the corner of a brick and concrete cover that they used to put over the cellar gratings. This was supposed to stop them getting a direct hit from the German bombers; fat lot of good it would have been if it had have got a hit. My eye was black and blue for ages, and the hat went into the miskin.

I had made mates with the gaffer's son from the Hen and Chickens who was in my class at school and I would run from our house, past the school to the pub, every day to escort him up the hill back to the school; the reason being that when I rang the bell for my mate, his dad would always give me a bag of Smith's crisps. It was heaven to eat the crisps sprinkled with the salt out of the little blue bags. In those tough times he was a friend worth cultivating.

We used to visit our dad who used to work with one of his brothers at his glass-blowing works, which was down an entry in Phillips Street, Aston. Dad and his brother Babs had worked for their Russian boss all their lives. Dad's other brother, Albert, was a professional soldier and had been in the Army since before the beginning of the Second World War. He had married a local girl and had a son called Derek. When he was home on leave they all lived in Phillips Street. Unfortunately, after fighting for five years, he was killed in action, and is buried at a place called Minterno in Italy. Mom used to say, "Our Albert got blowed up during the war", and I always thought Albert was her brother; it wasn't until years later that I found out he was my dad's brother. He had gone right through the war until 1944 and was fighting his way up Italy from the toe when his tank was blown to bits.

After the war Albert's wife remarried and they moved away from Aston to Kingstanding. Because of this, we lost touch with Derek and his mom and it wasn't until 2005 that we found each other again.

At the glassworks, dad and Babs made glass bowls and dishes, and the inevitable swans for neighbours and relatives; you weren't anybody if you didn't have a three-piece blue and white swan set in your house somewhere. Because of the heat from the furnaces, dad and his brother used to get through lots of liquids; they were always pleased when we went there to visit as it meant they could get us to fetch them some beer. The pub we used to go to was the Havelock on the main road. You took a couple of pop bottles to the "outdoor" and the barman filled them up with beer through a big copper tundish. He then stuck a sticker over the top of the bottle, and informed us that "no one under eighteen could drink the contents" on pain of imprisonment.

The glassworks was open all night and used to attract the local Bobbies who came in for a warm and a cup of tea. Once, my eldest brother had got pinched for having no lights on his bike and was fined ten bob; a fair bit of money back then. Anyway, he was with dad one night when the copper who nicked him walked in for a cup of tea. Needless to say, dad told him to sling his hook and never to come back again. Our dad and his brother worked in front of those furnaces for thirty hot, thirsty, dirty years, on permanent twelve-hour nights and for six nights a week. Neither of them had ever done anything else, and didn't want any other work. The end came in early 1953 when their boss just came in and said, "You are both finished the weekend"; no payout, no redundancy money, no dole money, no chance of getting any similar work — what a way to treat men after all those years of loyalty.

Our grandad and gran lived just up the road from the glassworks and we would sometimes call in on them when we visited dad. They lived down a yard and on their living room wall was a photo of a First World War regiment; grandad, who was gran's second husband, told us she had lost three of her sons in this war. On the outside wall was a piece of iron bar bent like a horseshoe; grandad had bent this when he was younger in a show of strength to some of the local kids.

The rent on our little palace was seven shillings and sixpence a week; not a lot of money in these days, but there were times when mom struggled to find the money to pay it. One day, when the rent man called, our mom hid on the stairs and said, "Tell him I'm not in". So when he knocked on the door I said "Mom said she is not in". "OK" was the reply, "tell her when she gets back off the stairs I'll call next week." The rent man was a man to be feared; he had the power to get you moved out of the area if he thought you were not up to scratch.

One word from him about the kids playing up or the garden or communal toilets not being clean or tidy led to feverish cleaning and head slapping until he was satisfied. During the long, drawn-out nights, we would listen to *Dick Barton: Special Agent, Lost in Space,* and *The Man in Black* on the radio; when we couldn't afford to get the accumulators our mom would sit us around the fire and get us to make up our own stories. She would start a sentence and we would have to supply a word that she would then use — the stories led to some weird and wonderful places, and none of them connected to a little slum house in Nechells.

To get us out for a day on a coach, our mom made me and my two sisters join the little church hall down in Long Acre. We would go there for Bible readings and hymn-singing, but the main reason for joining, though, was that we paid them three pence a week each and after six weeks you would qualify for a Sunday outing. Of course once you had been for the day out, you no longer went there — the three pence being more valuable elsewhere.

Christmas was always special: we would get out the trimmings that were made of coloured strips of paper glued into hooped chains, a bit of tinsel, a lot of coloured glass balls made by dad, and that was it. No Christmas tree, just a row of nails in the mantelpiece to hang up your sock and hope for the best. On reflection, Christmas presents always seemed to be the same — a torch with batteries that wouldn't last a day, a tin six-shooter complete with caps, an apple, an orange, nuts — and one year, at the bottom of our bed, a real wooden tank for me. This green man-made tank was the best in the world; it could go anywhere on its tracks which were beer bottle tops nailed to the sides. This tank lasted a couple of months, before, in the interests of warmth, it was broken up and used as fire wood.

Up our street was a little shop that used to sell all sorts of items, and once a year there would be a day when the sweets were off ration. This meant you could buy rocks, kali, sherbets, gobstoppers and all kinds of sweets without the dreaded ration book. This book was a treasure and without it you could hardy buy anything. The shopkeeper would put a cross in a little square in the book and when they were filled up that was it: no more of that item till the next ration book appeared.

Some people were so poor that they used to sell pages of their ration books to people who could afford them. It's sad, but we all felt a bit better off than these poor souls: you don't feel so bad when there is someone poorer than you. By the sweet shop lived a man who used to perform strongman acts in the Bull Ring. I made friends with his son, who took me to his house one dinner-time where his dad gave me some sausages and chips plastered with salt — I can't eat sausages or chips to this day without salt and it always brings back the same memory.

Horses and carts went along Rupert Street and Cromwell Street pulling their great loads down to the railway yards at the bottom of Cromwell Street. One day a year in May the carters would trim up their horses and parade them round the streets. The great shire horses were magnificent when they were decked out in their brasses and red, white and blue bunting. One day, at the top of our street, there had been an accident and I remember the horse lying on the ground with one of the shafts speared through it. It was making a terrible racket and died in great agony before the vet could get there. The carters would often park up their trusty steed while they had a pint or two in the local pub. They would put the nosebag on the horse and leave them to it. We used to hang around outside the pub and every once in a while a horse would have a pee — when it did so, one of the braver lads among us would throw chaff onto the extended member, thus effectively stopping it from being withdrawn. The driver would come back to his cart to find his horse standing there looking all forlorn with its chaff-covered thingy hanging there. A splash of water to wash away the offending bits and pieces, and all would be well once again. Cruel now, but fun then.

The milkman and the baker both drove horse-drawn carts, and if you were quick you could hang onto the springs by the back wheels and get a free ride. Me and my mate were on the back of the baker's cart one day in Cromwell Street, hanging on for dear life. When I looked at my mate, he was letting his hand run over the spokes of the wheel. Not to be outdone, I said "watch this!" and put my foot out to do what he was doing; a major mistake. In an instant my leg was caught in the spokes and jammed up between the wheel rim and the cart side. Luckily the road was made of cobbles, and the cart swung around and stopped in the gutter. My loyal mate was gone in a flash and I was left hanging there blarting my eyes out. It took three men to free me; they had to support my body and back up the horse to pull the wheel backwards off my leg. The second my feet hit the ground I was gone, running towards home with the shouts of the onlookers following me. I don't know how it happened but I was not injured apart from a small scar on the side of my leg. Lesson learned, I never attempted it again.

We were so poor that every so often my dad would send me around the streets to pick up fag ends. Up Charlie Arthur, left into Long Acre, and left again into Rocky Lane. Quite a few of these fag ends were found by the two number eight bus stops in Rocky Lane, but there were many trodden-on and flattened dog ends picked from the pavement and gutter. When I gave them to him he used to pull them apart and roll the tobacco into new fags.

Sometimes the trip would include Nechells Park Road with its factories, one of which had large bullet holes in its walls where it had been strafed by German fighters. My mom used to say she saw the pilot grinning as he shot up the area, but I think that was probably poetic licence. What wasn't poetic licence was the bomb peck on Nechells Green opposite the Beehive pub, where some houses and the occupants had been blown up. It was a place where I would spend hours playing in the dirt and bits of rubble. The chain from an old spring bed made a marvellous train as you dragged it through the dust. As kids we never realised that people had been killed on this spot; it was just a great place to play. Past the Beehive there was a bridge over the railway, and there were tales of kids who would lie between the tracks and let the trains run over the top of them. This road ran down to the Saltley gas works, where you could queue up for hours for half a hundredweight of coke. I can remember standing for hours waiting to be served; the bloke would put a sack under a chute and fill it to the proper weight — it was then up to you to get it home. You could hire a little cart with tiny cast-iron wheels to carry your load in, but these cost three pence, and of course you had to take it back, which meant another long trip in the cold. Most people either carried or dragged their wet, smelly bags with their precious load back home.

★   ★   ★

Our mom had lost the top half of her right index finger under a power press while making munitions. She received no sympathy as it was judged to be her own fault. There was no compensation and she was back at work two weeks later. When she was dozing in the armchair by the fire, this stump of the finger would twitch as if it had a life of its own. I asked her one day how it had happened and she said she had sneezed while picking her nose, which was why I shouldn't pick *my* nose. When our mom wasn't at munitions work, she would listen to the radio while doing her household chores, and every so often I heard her say "ahmybing"; I could never figure out what an "ahmybing" was. It turned out that she would say this phrase when Bing Crosby came on the radio, and what she was really saying was, "Ah my Bing". Another of her sayings was "hardened bark"; this was generally aimed at anyone who wouldn't do as they were told. All my dad ever seemed to say was "that kid's got a kink", as he pointed to me.

Our mom was great. She was as fair as circumstances allowed her to be, and woe betide anyone who bought shame on our house. One day I had played wag from Cromwell Street School with my mate. We hadn't gone far, just across the road playing on a bombed peck. The headmaster sent out my sister to fetch us but we wouldn't go back with her. That night at home my mom sent me to the shop in Nechells Park Road to buy a three penny bamboo stick; when I got back to the house my mom sent my two sisters out to bring back a couple of mates each. When this group of people had assembled, she whipped down my short trousers and with the bamboo stick gave me the whacking of my life on my bare arse. I still have the scars to this day, but I never played wag again until I was fifteen.

One time our mom had saved up enough money to buy a tin of cocoa, an almost unheard of luxury. She then found out that someone had been using the cocoa and that half had gone. She made us all gather round in the room and questioned us until she found out who the culprit was; it turned out to be one of my brothers. When she confirmed this she took the tin with the remaining cocoa in it and threw it in his face saying, "You may as well have the lot". Likewise, when one of my sisters bought a bag of aniseed balls home and wouldn't share them, mom said, "Let's have a look at them". When she was shown the sweets, she knocked the bag into the air and we all scrambled to get as many as we could. They may have been covered in fluff and God knows what else, but they tasted great. A salutary lesson to all of us about share and share alike.

Money was so scarce that when our mom wanted to go out she would give me a little bag and tell me to ask the builders down the road to fill it with sand. When I gave it to her she would take some out, get it wet and rub it on her legs; this made her look like she had nylon stockings on, and her friend, who she would go out with, made her stand on the table and then drew a line down the back of her legs with a black eyeliner pencil. Tough times require tough solutions.

My middle brother who was mom's favourite was in the Scouts. He had all the right gear: hat, knife, uniform, and a six-foot pole — he really looked the part, and he took it very seriously. His hat, which was obviously a hand-me-down from within the Scouting fraternity, was miles too big. But mom had the answer: she filled the rim inside with newspaper so that although it looked enormous on the outside, when he put it on it was a snug fit. This worked alright till one night it poured down with rain, and when he came home his face, unknown to him, was covered with black ink stains. No one had told him at the Scouts meeting and he was really upset when we all laughed at him. Our mom used to say, "he ain't got a big head", and in the next breath, amid gales of laughter, would tell him to go to the grocer's and get ten pound of spuds in his hat. He came home one night with his stick in two pieces, a black eye and scratches down his legs; he and his mates had been vaulting over people's fences when his stick had broken in mid-flight, causing him to land in a hedge. He was mortified on two counts: one because his mates couldn't stop laughing, and two because mom couldn't afford to get him another stick.

Across our yard was a man who had been a soldier in India during the war, and above his mantelpiece, in pride of place, was a photograph of him holding a monkey in front of the Taj Mahal. I thought this photo was magnificent and would spend ages just looking at it. I always longed to have my photo taken in that same place, and many, many years later I achieved this goal. I'll bet not many people who had their photo taken in front of that awe-inspiring building were thinking of a little back-to-back house where a long-dead soldier used to live, when the shutter went "click".

At the end of the war we had a victory party in our street and there were tables right across the horse road. There was no problem with traffic because nobody had a car. There were trimmings pinned to the walls and around the windows, and above the entries there was the V sign painted in red, white and blue. All the horses were trimmed up like it was May Day. Everybody said we had won the war, and there was great rejoicing but it never seemed to alter our lives one bit. The rationing still continued and you still had to queue for ages in the wet and cold to get anything to eat. The arse was out of your bags and your socks had spuds in them — I remember my shorts being held up by threadbare braces for years. I was fourteen before I got my first pair of long trousers, and underpants were unheard of, skid-marks being the order of the day for most kids. Our mom sometimes used to barter the clothing coupons out of her ration book for food coupons. We never had any money to buy new clothes anyway. If we were in need of any clothes, shoes or whatever, our mom would say, "It's time to go to 'Sally Anne's' "; this was the Salvation Army's room up by Gosta Green. There was a big hall and all the people had to sit down and be quiet, then the people on the stage, mostly ladies, would hold up items of clothing that had been donated to the Salvation Army by the better-off citizens of Brum. You then had to bid for whatever article you wanted, the cry being "here you are, miss, a penny for this, or tuppence for that". You could get almost anything for three pence: clothes, shoes, toys — and when you got home you would be dressed in some really weird and wonderful clothes.

Occasionally mom and dad would take us on a day out to the Lickeys. Amid great excitement for us kids, she would make up some sandwiches; these were usually bread and lard, liberally sprinkled with salt and pepper. Drinks were a milk bottle full of cold tea. Was there ever better fare in all the world? We would get the bus to town and make our way to Navigation Street to join all the other would-be happy travellers. The queue for the trams sometimes went along Navigation Street round the corner and all the way up Hill Street, such was the pull of the Lickeys. No jumping in, you just waited your turn and remained patient. A bone-rattling ride took you along the middle of the Bristol road, the tracks running between the conker trees, the branches of which used to scrape along the side of the tram as it progressed. Arriving at the terminus, the tram would disgorge its teeming passengers, the conductor would swing the arm around on the top with a big pole and off it would go to collect another happy band. On getting off the tram our dad would invariably head for the Hare and Hound, with the words: "I'll see you by so-and-so place in an hour or so".

Nothing that we knew of could compare with the Lickeys. For young kids from the slums it had everything: trees to climb, and play hide-and-seek among, slopes to slide down, little lakes, a tea shop, fresh air, free from the smell of factory chimneys that spewed out obnoxious fumes day and night, and if and when it was a clear day, and you climbed to the top of the hills, there were wonderful views of the chimney stacks, the gasometers, and the empty spots where the German bombers had flattened the buildings of Brum. If you were lucky you could find frogs and newts in the little streams that flowed off the hills. If you did, it wasn't much of a life for them cooped up in a jam jar or a cardboard box. After a day of rolling down hills, hide-and-seeking, climbing, playing cowboys and Indians, and pinching the occasional golf ball, it would be time to go. This time the queues would stretch for hundreds of yards, only this time it was made up of tired moms, nervous dads and snot-nosed kids blowing green bubbles as they blarted and moaned about being tired and the like. Yes, if you were a kid there was no better place on earth than the Lickeys. We Brummies may not have had a lot but what we did have we really enjoyed, and we all shared it together.

When I was about six or seven we went on a week's camping holiday to Bewdley. This was like going to the ends of the earth for us kids; we got on the bus to town and then the Midland Red, and set off on our epic voyage. The length of the trip proved too much for our dad's bladder, having had a few prior to getting on board. So with no further ado, he said to the driver, "You'd better stop mate 'cos I need to pee"; everyone on board heard this request and our mom was mortified, but the driver did stop and I can see our dad now (as could all on board) as he stood behind a farm wall resplendent in his trilby hat happily letting nature take its course. Passing Webb's, which back then was only a big house and some fields full of flowers, we arrived to be picked up by a lorry that took us the final mile or so to the campsite. On the way we passed fields with rabbits all over them; the sight of these rabbits amazed me because the only time I had ever seen rabbits was when they were hanging up on butcher's hooks, or stewing in a pot. Cows and sheep were equally as strange to me. On the subject of rabbits, our mom could make a rabbit last three days, stewed in a big black pot that hung over the fire. She would just keep adding bits of vegetables and things — not much fear of being overfed in those days. This campsite was in a field below the railway line and at night you could hear the steam train blowing its whistle as it came up the Severn Valley, its fire lighting up the clouds and the belching steam looked bright red and pink as it swept along. If you went on one of these noisy, snorting, hissing trains, the best way to travel was with your head out of the drop-down window; this made sure you had the best view, but you had to watch for approaching trains if you looked out of the line-side windows. Bits of coal dust would sometimes get in your eyes, and you always got off the train with a chimney sweep's face, with white eyes and mouth and hair that stuck up like a ventriloquist's dummy. If you travelled any sort of distance on a steam train, the clacking sound of the wheels on the lines would make you want to sleep.

Another trip that we used to take, which our mom said was a reward for us being good, but which was probably to get us out of her way, was all the way round on the number eight bus. Our mom would take us to the bus stop in Rocky Lane, pay the tuppence each that it cost for this trip and tell the conductor to take us all the way round. This trip would last approximately two hours, and if you were quick enough you could get the front seat upstairs and "drive" the bus by steering with the handrail. This all the way round trip must have been the best value for money you could imagine. It certainly kept us happy and you could nose into other people's gardens and windows as you swept by. On the number eight you passed the Saltley gas works, the Morris car works, Hughes's biscuit factory, the Waldorf skating rink and the inevitable bomb pecks. One time, my mate John and me decided to go down to Saltley on the bus. We only had a penny between us so me being the smallest I sat on John's lap and when the conductor asked for the fare John said, "One to Saltley gas works". "How about him?" asked the conductor, pointing at me, "he's only four, so I don't have to pay for him", was the reply. The bus, which was full of people going to work, erupted with laughter and the conductor, who must have been a kindly soul, let us get away with it.

Because our mom was on essential war work, I, like lots of others, was taken to Cromwell Street School during the day, even though I was only about three at the time. In the afternoons they would get out camp beds and expect you to have a sleep for a couple of hours — some hope in a room full of two- to four-year-olds! A few things stand out in my mind about these times; one was when the whole class had painted their favourite scenes on a long piece of rolled out white paper on the floor. We had all done a part of this, and the teacher was about to invite other children in the school to view these works of art when, for some reason, I apparently decided I could leap over this obstacle. I didn't quite make it and the work of art with its cowboys and Indians, its Spitfires and bombers, and its animals was ripped completely through the middle. I can't remember the punishment, but I'm sure it fitted the crime. After the unsuccessful leaping like a gazelle incident, I was apparently a person not to be seen mixing with. I remember feeling ostracised by my classmates, until one day a little red-haired girl called Barbara came and sat by me and put her arm around me, and in that one small gesture of friendliness and warmth which no one else had ever shown me, I fell in love forever both with Barbara, and redheads in general. At school we would sit around in groups and when one of the minders asked us what we wanted to be when we grew up I said I wanted to be the "cowboy with a banjo on his knee", mainly because he always rode off into the western sunset on his trusty steed.

You would pass the barber's on the way to school, his shop being on the hill in Rocky Lane. I remember that he had pictures on his shop wall of racing drivers, and he would make you kneel on the seat when it was your turn for a haircut. I don't think this bloke liked kids too much, because if you squirmed with the pain of this Chinese-type torture, or didn't turn your head the way he wanted it, he would flick your ear with his finger, which was painful, and if that didn't make you toe the line, a sharp nip with clippers certainly would.

One clear afternoon when we were all supposed to be asleep on the camp beds, we became aware of a deep rumbling sound, and loose things in the room began to rattle slightly. I remember it was a clear sunny day, and our minders must have thought it was important because they took us outside to show us what was happening. Looking up into the sky, there were hundreds of tiny silver planes flying in formation; what a sight for little kids whose whole lives so far had been dominated by visions of war — a dream come true. I don't know to this day if it was one of the thousands of bomber raids that were pretty common by then heading for Germany, or perhaps the invasion of Europe. Whatever it was, it is as clear in my mind now as it was then.

I would go to this school in my little wellington boots, turned right down so that I could run faster. That there was no embarrassment in wearing these things to school in the summer was a real sign of the times, and most people had weird and wonderful footwear in those days. It was about this time that our mom's brother came to stay with us. Me and mom were at home one cold, wet and windy day when the front door was knocked. On opening it, there was mom's brother, stood in the pouring rain in his trilby hat and raincoat running with water. He had a sodden bag in one hand and an old suitcase in the other. "She's thrown me out, our May", were the only words he said, in a choked voice. "You'd better come in then", said mom without any hesitation at all. It seems that when it was found out he had TB, that killer of the poor, which, due to the wet, damp and poor diet of most of the slummies, was rife, and he couldn't work any more, his wife had shown him the door. Uncle stopped with us until the day he died, and although he could add very little to the house in a financial sense, he brought his own sense of humour and kindness with him, and I never heard him raise his voice or lose his temper once. He always seemed to have a pack of cards in his hands and could do all sorts of tricks. He used to say, "I can feel the spots on the cards", and if you chose a card he was able to tell you what it was. Another of his sayings which I found hard to fathom out was if we were going out at the same time he would say, "If you get back first you put a brick on the window sill, if I get back first I'll take it off". Because of his illness he used to have a little bottle with him, supplied by the hospital. He carried this at all times, and every time he had a coughing fit and would retch up phlegm, he would spit it into the bottle. I suppose this was essential in the fight against TB, but it could be a little off-putting during mealtimes. He died of this terrible disease in 1953 in a bedroom I shared with him over the chemist's shop in Summer Lane. In the end a nurse came in every day to clean him and check him over. One day I heard her say to our mom, "He's as tough as old boots". He lasted six weeks without food, his yellow filmed-over eyes that couldn't shut by now, staring straight ahead. I would ask him if he wanted a piece of toast or something, and during this time he always

25

called me by my brother's name, who had been a favourite of his. They only moved me out of the room when he got the death rattle. I suppose they thought it was not the best thing for a twelve-year-old to hear. The council sent in people to spray the room with some sort of disinfectant, which stank for weeks. This was a very sad death which was unfortunately shared by all too many families back then. The only redeeming thing about this terrible affair was that he was surrounded by loving relatives when he passed away — although he probably never knew it.

One day in 1947 a strange white light coming through the bedroom window woke our mom. The other reason for her getting up was that dad hadn't got home yet — this was most unusual. I heard her getting up and got up with her and we went downstairs past the lurking bucket. Strangely, downstairs was darker than the bedrooms and mom decided to open the front door to see what was the matter. When she opened the door we were confronted by a wall of snow from the front step to the top of the door. The snow had been coming down all night and had drifted up against all the houses in our terrace. Luckily, although it was high, it was not too deep and we soon dug ourselves out to freedom — what an adventure for a six-year-old! I felt as if I was Flash Gordon and that Ming had walled me into a snowy tomb. During the day we were able to get around a bit because people had dug pathways from the houses towards the street. I vanished and went to see if Cromwell Street School was open. The caretaker, who had dug a path from the front gate to the school and was obviously tired, told me to sod off. During the following weeks the snow slowly melted and left behind it fantastic icicles which hung off every roof and projection. Some of these icicles were bigger than me and if they had dropped on you they could have caused a lot of damage. Some of the buildings looked as if they were protected by glass prison bars. They were also great ice-lollies if you could stand the coldness of them.

If you walked down Long Acre towards Salford Park on the right by Cuckoo Bridge was a little gravelled area called Spion Kop. This had been a gun emplacement during the war, built no doubt to protect the local factories, and was a huge mound made of soil. This hill was great for sliding and rolling down when being shot in either a game of cowboys and Indians, or soldiers. I had my first ride on a big sit-up-and-beg bike here. It was too big for me to sit on the saddle and pedal, but I managed by riding on the crossbar. Getting excited at my new-found prowess, I immediately fell off it when trying to ride with only one hand holding the handlebars, resulting in more scratches and bruises. As you went over the hump-backed Cuckoo Bridge there was a wooden gate leading onto the cut. I would sometimes go there with a mate of mine who lived nearby, whose parents had been bargees. If you went along the towpath you could get to Salford Viaduct, where the kids who lived local to the cut used to swim there naked. Sometimes we would be lucky enough to catch sight of the wonderfully painted barges low down in the water, full of coal or other materials sailing quietly by, pulled by their horses with their brass buckles and badges glinting and glittering in the sun. All the little hump-backed bridges over the cut had deep furrows cut into the stonework caused over the years by the ropes as the horses went over them. It would be fascinating for us to watch the barges go through the locks, and we were always willing to lend a hand to turn the lock keys that filled or emptied them with water. It seemed to me to be a great way to live, slowly gliding through the ever-changing scenery of the Midlands canals. Self-contained and as free as a bird, I didn't realise for many years that the people who lived and worked on the barges had a really hard, tough life.

CHAPTER
TWO

Moving House

By early 1949 our house had reached bursting point with us kids getting bigger and the rooms seemingly getting smaller. Our mom, who had been badgering the council for a change of house, finally got her wish. We got a bigger house in a place called Summer Lane. I had never heard of it but mom was delighted; she had been born in Gee Street, which was off Summer Lane and said she felt like she was going home. Moving anything in those days was easy; all you had to do was to hire a big cart with two big wheels like the ones the carters used to sell their fruit and vegetables from in the Bull Ring. You then loaded your furniture onto this cart and pushed it to wherever you wanted to go. This is what we did; we went up Rocky Lane along to Aston Cross, down to Phillips Street down Aston Brooke Street, up Newtown Row into Cowper Street, and up to the chemist shop on the corner of Cowper Street and Summer Lane: and all this with me carrying a chair. We must have looked a real sight, but we only took two loads to move all our belongings, and we finally got to our new home. Compared to Poplar Terrace this place was a palace. It was over the chemist's shop so had the same size rooms above, and they were huge. The bedroom I slept in held three beds and still looked empty. One of my sisters lived in the room above the shop with her husband and daughter. There was a kitchen and even a bathroom; the bath wasn't used though, and we kept coal in it, preferring to carry on using the tin bath we had always used. Some habits are hard to break! The hot water was obtained by boiling saucepans and the kettle. If, like me, you were the youngest, you had the last bath, and by that time the water had taken on a distinctly grey colour, but it didn't seem to do me any harm.

When we first moved in, the rooms had bare floorboards, and if it rained the water ran down some of the walls. Little blue flashes could be seen and you got a tingle of electricity running up your arm when you turned the brass light switch on. Being over the chemist's shop, everything that came into the house had to be carried upstairs. Chairs, tables, settees were all got up and around the corner at the top. Our mom could play the piano and had always wanted one, and moving into this bigger place meant there was room for a piano. God only knows how the blokes got this piano, which must have weighed a ton, up those stairs and around the corner. But they did and that piano went on for many a year and at many a party. The room my brother, uncle and I slept in overlooked both Cowper Street and Summer Lane. The Summer Lane view included a bombed peck and the Three Horse Shoes pub — one of about eighteen that used to be in Summer Lane from the bottom of Snow Hill to Asylum

Road. This pub was as well used as any other in the lane, and was full every weekend. Fights were fairly frequent, and, quivering with excitement, I used to watch the punch-ups from my bedroom. Generally it would be two blokes squaring up to each other with perhaps a few mates watching; no knives, no bottles, just straight-out raw guts. If a bloke was knocked down he was let back up to his feet to carry on, and if and when the fight finished, the first man to buy the loser a pint was the man who had just beaten him. Music was generally provided by the travelling accordion players who would either stand outside the pub or open the latch and put their foot in to keep the door open. Sing-songs would happen most Saturday and Sunday nights, with or without the travelling musicians. Opposite the pub and just a little way up Cowper Street was a coal yard, where queues of people desperate for coal would form in all sorts of weather. We were lucky living across the road because we could just keep an eye on things and go for coal when it was quiet. The bloke who ran this coal yard must have been an ex-Army wallah because he was forever telling people to get in line, and ordering people about. Some people are never happy unless they are shouting and bawling. Coal would be weighed in a large container shaped like a big coal scuttle and it was then either put into sacks or straight into your preferred form of transport. This transport could be weird and wonderful — anything from an old pram, the crossbar of a bike, a four-wheeled plank, or if you could afford it, the coal yard cart with its painted number and inevitable small cast-iron wheels, which were a swine to get up and down the pavements. Up this end of Cowper Street lived a girl whose family had the very first TV set I had ever seen. I made friends with her and got to see this wonder of the modern age; a grainy black-and-white showing of an opera was on view that particular day. I was with the girl one day when she pushed me over; there was no malice involved, I just happened to fall, but in doing so I dislocated my little finger. The finger stuck out at a strange angle and looked really queer. Back home, my mom made a sling out of an old tie and sent me to the hospital with my big brother, who moaned all the way there because he had better things to do. When we got to see the doctor he took one look at this strangely angled digit, got hold of it, asked me to look out of the window, and in one swift painless movement, pulled it back into its proper place. "That's it", he told my brother. I was really disappointed. I had been expecting a plastered arm complete with sling, and a few days off school to recuperate — no such luck.

The windows of our house looking into Cowper Street were opposite a large house and small engineering shop. This workshop was in what had been the garage of the house; there were lathes and drilling machines, and three or four blokes worked in there. There were probably hundreds of these little engineering shops across Brum; it must have been where the saying "city of a thousand trades" came from. Down that side of the street were all the yards with their terraced houses, and when we first moved there the brick-built bomb shelters were still standing. Not for these people the underground bomb-proof cellars. Live or die on the streets seemed to be the order of the day. On our side was that great old school, Cowper Street, with its steeple-like tower and its pointed roofs.

Thousands and thousands of kids must have gone through those old green wrought iron gates into the school playground; a large area of black tarmac and not a blade of grass to be seen. The teachers, given the circumstances and the abject poverty of their pupils, did an outstanding job. They were hard but fair, and gave most of the kids a good grounding for the future. I have never heard anyone say a bad thing about Cowper Street, which is a living testament to the selfless, hard-working, caring nature of its teachers.

Being the new kid in the street, I had to find my place in the local hierarchy, and this was done by having to fight nearly every kid in the street. These fights were always one to one, with no outside interference from either kids or adults. No kicking, no hair-pulling, just straight-out punching with the occasional wrestling move thrown in. The winner was decided by one or the other of the fighters giving in; there was never any shame in this as long as you had done your best. The final move of the punch-up was invariably the assailants walking away with their arms around each other's shoulders into the sunset, declaring they were mates for life. My mom must have known what was going on but she never made any comments, and I never said anything about the black eyes and bruises — she just used to clean them up as best as she could. Anyway, after a few black eyes, scratches and bruises, I was finally accepted as one of the Cowper Street gang. This was important because we used to have fights which consisted mainly of throwing taunts and stones at each other with similar gangs of ragged-arsed heroes from the surrounding streets. These epic battles were generally fought out on the bombed peck on the corner of Ormond Street and Summer Lane. The hoardings that tried to hide this rubble-strewn area from the delicate sight of the drinkers in the Birmingham Arms was anything you wanted it to be: a ship's sails, a rock face, or castle walls. One of the games would be to jump off the hoardings from as high as you dared, and many a pirate or commando went home to mom with a sprained ankle. Just down Ormond Street from this bombed peck there was a blacksmith's shop; you could stand and watch him fitting horseshoes to the massive horses, as long as you were quiet. How he handled these large beasts was a sight to be seen. It was fascinating to see him fashion a shoe out of a flat piece of metal; the smoke and smell that came off the hooves as he tried the shoes was terrible. The smithy would vanish in a foul-smelling cloud of yellow smoke, then emerge to plunge the red-hot shoe into a bucket of water. We would try to get hold of the bits of hoof that he had trimmed off. These little off-cuts had an amazing attraction for dogs; if you could, you would try to drop a piece down someone's trouser turn-ups and follow them to see what happened.

When they demolished St Stephen's Church at the bottom of Cowper Street on Newtown Row it was the end of an era for us kids. The church had been in a really bad state of repair, and when Newtown Row was modernised it had to come down. This was a shame because although I don't remember anyone going to the church to pray, there would be crowds of kids going along to see the "flicks" that Father Blood would show. These films featuring Laurel and Hardy, Charlie Chaplin and the like could be seen down in the cellars or crypts for the princely sum of tuppence. You were made to sit on the kneeling pads that were brought down from the church above. When we had all shut up shouting and talking the projectionist would start the magic lantern. The soundless black and white flickering screen would hold our attention until the inevitable breakdown. This would be greeted with roars of disapproval, especially if it happened at an exciting time. It was local, it was cheap and it was great fun. It was while playing in the ruins of the church that I met my best mate; he lived at the bottom of Cowper Street, but was regarded a little suspiciously by our mob because he wasn't allowed to play with us roughs. He was forever dressed in home-made knitted jumpers, whatever the weather, and was always clean and tidy. He seemed to have nice new toys, and the *Dandy* and *Beano* straight from the shop. In a world of second-hand things these were other reasons to be distrustful. No image of a mommy's boy could be further from the truth — he was fearless in a fight and would take on all-comers, big or small. He could bird nest with the best of us and would climb trees like a monkey. He had absolutely no nerves at all when it came to playing dangerous games and certainly warranted his place in the gang when he was finally allowed to mix with us. For some long-forgotten reason we were paired together for a fight, and I have to say he beat me hands down, one of the very few people who ever did. This scrap only reinforced our friendship which lasted for a good many years after.

The fight had taken place in Blews Street Park, which was across Newtown Row and just down St Stephen's Street. This Disneyworld of its time had a few swings, a roundabout, and a witch's hat. A concrete and gravel floor, great for scrages, and not a blade of grass to be seen. But what an attraction to the local kids: the roundabout would be sent spinning like a demented dervish, and woe betide any kid whose skinny little arms couldn't keep him on board. Those who couldn't hang on were thrown off yards away, tearing both clothes and skin in equal amounts on the unforgiving gravel and there was many a black eye obtained by walking into one or other of the swings. It seemed that everyone's ambition who got on the swings was to turn it right over the top. Likewise with the witch's hat, this was cranked around and around at far greater speeds than it was ever intended to achieve, squealing its disapproval as it did so. Sandwiched between factories, grim terraced houses, and the Miller Street tram depot, it was a great place for us kids.

When they tore up Newtown Row, part of the road was found to be made of wooden blocks. Over the years these had soaked up countless gallons of oil and tons of horse droppings and were covered by black tar. This made them burn like coal and in no time there were dozens and dozens of adults and kids ripping up these blocks. Me and my mates would sell them for a tanner a bag; they tried to stop us by having a night watchman, but he was just as skint as us and would turn a blind eye. Not that he would have been able to stop the hordes of cash-strapped kids anyway. Whenever I smell burning tar, it brings back those memories of an open fire with wooden blocks burning merrily in the grate. And black-faced kids tearing up the horse road.

We made our own enjoyment with loads of games, spinning tops, hopscotch and skipping for the girls, glarneys in the gutter, hide and seek, football, pretend fighting and races, etc. for the boys. Hide-and-seek was a popular game in the dark nights because you had the cover of darkness to help you. It was during one of these games that my nose was flattened for a second time. I had been lying on top of a wall in the pitch dark when someone came from nowhere and shoved me head first onto the blue bricks of the next yard. The crack of my nose and the stars I saw were horrendous — my nose burst like a tomato. I wouldn't let them take me home in case I got in trouble with our mom, so they took me to a lady who was pretty good with injuries. There, for the second time in my short life, I once again had my nose straightened. I had two real shiners for weeks, and although I knew who the pusher was, he never admitted it, and him being bigger than me, I never pursued the matter. One of the games we played consisted of leap-frogging over two dustbins; these were placed on the pavement outside the school. The distances apart were determined by the amount of blue bricks between each bin. These blue bricks were about four inches wide, so if you had six bricks and the bins were two feet wide that would be about six feet you had to go over. One day things were really hotting up and it had come down to two lads as to who would be the best. They had both gone over twelve bricks, so the miskins were pretty far apart. One of the bigger kids appeared from up his yard and wanted to know who was doing what; when he was told he took over the spacing of the bins. He didn't like one of the lads so when it was his turn, and without him saying anything, he pushed the bins to sixteen bricks apart. This lad came flying down the street all whirling arms and legs resembling a demented storm-driven windmill, his hob-nailed boots striking sparks as he got up speed, and he then took off like a startled gazelle and cleared the bins as gracefully as any gymnast could ever have done. There was a massive roar of both glee and disappointment: glee because he had done the impossible, disappointment because he had done it. We had all expected to see him fall flat on his face. He was amazed to find himself the hero of all the little kids in street, and was equally gobsmacked when he was told of the amount of bricks between the bins. Needless to say this feat was never repeated and went down as a legend in the street's history. These miskins and their lids used to take a terrible hammering in the days around bonfire night: a penny banger stuck under a lid on the pavement could lift it twenty feet into the air they were so powerful. If you put one of these deadly bangers in a milk bottle it would blow it apart. If your boots had studs in them you could slide around on the brick pavements; it was difficult to get up speed but when you did you could slide a really long way.

When we got a bit bolder we would take down a clothes-line and tie up the doorknobs of the back doors of two or three of the houses; a knock on the door and a rush to hide and then watch the fun as each pulled their door in turn trying to open it. Finally someone would come out the front door and round the back to release the clothes-line. Curses and threats of death and all sorts would make you tingle in fear as you chewed on your coat sleeve to stop laughing. Up one of the yards there was a brick wall which was easy to climb; this was the back wall of a hall that was in Ormond Street. If you climbed up the drainpipe of this building you could get onto the roofs of the houses in the yard. One night me and my mate who had been told off that day by one of the long-suffering residents decided to wreak revenge on the poor soul. We didn't really have a plan of action, but we climbed onto his roof. Once there, hanging onto his smoking chimney, we decided to block it. We pulled a couple of slates off the roof and put them over the chimney pot and scuttled off the roof. Hiding in the toilets down the yard, we heard him shouting, "Fire, fire!", and looking up the yard he had got all his family out in the cold. The smoke was billowing out of his back door. The fire brigade came and put the fire out, but it wasn't until he got the chimney sweep in the following day that he found out that there had been slates put over his chimney pots. Strangely, he didn't seem to bother us too much after that. Another trick was to balance milk bottles on the brass doorknobs of three or four houses then knock the door and run. You would hear the first bottle smash, followed swiftly by the others as people came out to see what the row was all about. This time it would be the lady of the house who cursed you; she, like all people in all houses everywhere, had probably spent hours on her hands and knees scrubbing the step and polishing it red with Cardinal polish, and to have milk bottles and milk smashed over it would not have been funny. The cleaning of these doorsteps was a must for most of the families who lived in our street. It showed you were a clean family and proud of your little house. The window cleaner was also an essential person because no matter how hard people tried they could not stop the film of dirt from the surrounding factories and the coal fires settling on the window-panes and making the insides of the houses even gloomier.

Cowper Street School, although it had a big green spear-topped iron fence surrounding it, was easy to get into; we would just go straight over the top of the fence. My mate and I found that if you got onto the first roof by climbing up a drainpipe, you could then get right up to the main roof. We had found that there was a gap of about a yard between the chimney and the tower that ran right up to the main roof. All you had to do was to put your feet on the one wall and your back on the other and slowly push your way to the top, just like Roy Rogers climbing a rock face. Once you were on the top of the ridges the view was terrific. We could see down to Lucas's at Hockley, the Barton's Arms and Hip, down Newtown Row, and even parts of town. But the main thing was we could see most of the houses in Cowper Street, and lots of the back houses in Ormond Street. We both had catapults and we would sit completely invisible in the dark on separate ridges about fifty foot off the ground and aim our catapults at our neighbours' doors. The ensuing mayhem this caused was hilarious to us. People running around trying to find the phantom door-knockers. There was no chance of seeing us above the gas lamps in the street. The school was also used for all sorts of meetings, and when it was, we were able to get into the yard and generally act like idiots. One night there was a political meeting of some sort and one of the hopeful future councillors had driven up in his little three-wheeled plastic car. These tiny cars were really like covered motorbikes and as such, were relatively light. Six of us lads picked this little vehicle up carried it into the schoolyard and deposited it in the outside toilet. All hell broke loose when the meeting ended with the poor victim running everywhere looking for his prized car. When he threatened to go to Bridge Street police station, he was eventually told where it was, and we gave him a hand to get it back onto the street. The man was so thankful he gave us a few bob for our troubles.

From this vantage point on the roof we could see the Three Horse Shoes; this pub was on the corner of

Summer Lane and Cowper Street, and you would see all sorts of people in all sorts of states either stagger or walk straight out of this little hostelry. One such person was an old lady that lived up one of the yards. She was always dressed the same winter or summer, with a man's flat cap, a muffler and an old past-her-knees man's overcoat. We would watch her stagger and half run with a crab-like gait across the newly installed zebra crossing with its bright orange Belisha beacon on the top. On obtaining the safety of the opposite pavement, she would slowly stagger down the street, right arm rigidly stuck out, supporting herself off the walls as she went. This method of getting home was alright until she got to one of the many yard entries: then if she didn't realise she had got there, she would fall without a murmur onto the floor where she would remain until some kindly soul or other lifted her up and sent her on her way. If we kids were about and attempted to lift her, she would curse and swear at us no end. This expert use of obscenities, coming from a little old lady, would send us into gales of laughter, and spur her on to curse us all the more.

Although we lived in the middle of Aston with not a blade of grass in sight, and the only birds to be seen were sparrows and pigeons, the lads I got to know were some of the best little naturalists I ever met. There were lads who could tell what the clouds were and what they meant weather-wise; some seemingly knew every bird that flew. One of the lads could tell us what almost each plant was and whether you could eat it or not: I don't remember anyone eating any, though. When we went on expeditions to Perry Barr Park they could find birds' nests in minutes, and I was amazed at the first blackbirds' egg I saw, I had never imagined anything like it. Strict rules among us meant that only one egg would be taken from a nest, and in all my time with the gang I never saw this self-imposed rule broken. Some of these lads could find frogs and newts; Red House Park in Perry Common being a favourite place because it had a lake and our lads knew the time of the year to go frog-spawning. There was many a jar of tadpoles on window-sills in the tenement houses of Aston. One year when we had gone looking for frogs and newts, the whole lake was frozen over; the ice that covered the lake was as clear as glass, and after one brave soul proved it could be walked and slid upon, there was no stopping our little mob. The sights through the ice were great, long fronds of weeds, the sandy and muddy bottom with little whirls of muddy smoke where a fish or some other water creature had sped away from the giants above them; red and blue flashing sticklebacks, larger fish if you were quick and lucky enough, and because the ice was like a magnifying glass, water snails, water fleas and the occasional bike frame were easily spotted. These ragged-arsed kids from the depths of Aston, from the poorest of families, and from some of the worst living conditions you could imagine, only looked up to the skies and very rarely downwards. We didn't know any better and so we were happy with what we did have. If one of us had to walk home from Perry Barr or the Lickeys, which was not unusual, especially if you had spent your tram or bus fare, then we all walked. No one was better than his or her mates unless it was a self-achieved thing.

CHAPTER
THREE

The Onion Fair &
Other Stories

Once a year the Onion Fair would arrive down by
Aston Park. What a sight for kids starved of excitement:
bright-coloured lights, ear-shattering noises from diesel
and the steam engines used to power the rides, music
to blast your eardrums to bits. The smell of the petrol
and diesel fumes, the roast spuds, three pence a bag
and as much salt as you liked, the candyfloss, the
onions, rubber; it was like another fantastic world to us
kids. You could win anything you liked at the Onion
Fair provided it was a goldfish, a plaster of Paris dog, or
a day-old brightly coloured chick. There must have
been many a house in Brum that had its fish or fowl
winnings brought home by some happy little kid.
Feeding them though, with money always so short, was
another thing. In the boxing booths, the barker would
try to wind up the locals to get someone into the ring
with one of his many pugilists; these guys were an
awesome lot, flattened noses, cauliflower ears and scars
all over their faces. They ranged in size from little to
really large, and this being Aston and renowned for its

rough, tough image, there was always someone who would oblige. Generally the local hero would pick out the smallest bloke to have a go at. This was normally a huge mistake, as these lads had fought all sorts of people in all sorts of places and were quick, mobile, and very, very tough, The referee was an expert at letting his boxer know how to handle his opponent and he would slow him down at the beginning to make it look like our lad had got the better of him. The third round would have everyone screaming and yelling themselves hoarse for "our kid", but with a fiver at stake there was no way he would win, although when you did get the occasional upset, the ringmaster reluctantly paid out, trying to smile but looking as if he had drunk a pint of vinegar. The big wheel would take you above the heaving masses of humanity to a higher level; you went right above the chimney tops like a bird, the sights and sounds of the fairground receding downwards for a while. An oasis of calm in this madness of light and noise. The bumper cars were an absolute must for all kids of all ages; there were arrows on the side of the rink showing which way you were supposed to go, but this being Aston there was always someone or other who would chance his arm going against the flow. The tough-looking fairground workers who could in number appear from nowhere, soon bought these reprobates back into line. Teeth-rattling, bone-shaking, body-bruising rides under the blue crackling, sparking electric power system. Wonderful. The wall of death was another favourite, with its smell of rubber and engine fumes; the whizzing bikes would flash around like whirling dervishes. They would come right to the top of the rink trying to run over the fingers of anyone daft enough to put their hands over the edge with a roar that would deafen you for a while.

Most lads I knew would have a go at the coconut shy. This was to try to impress your mates, and more especially, any watching girls, that you were strong and could aim. You had a wooden ball and you were supposed to knock a coconut off its support, but these coconuts must have weighed a half hundredweight each because it was virtually impossible to shift them: even when you had a direct hit with all your force behind it these things barely moved. Not being able to dislodge these cast-iron coconuts spurred you on to greater efforts, much to the amusement of the watching crowd and not many blokes walked away with a coconut from that place. There was the helter-skelter for the littler kids and the waltzers for the bigger, braver ones. These instruments of fun spun round at a G-force that would keep you pinned to your seat, and all the time being twisted violently by the sadistic helpers! These blokes would walk around and through the madly spinning waltzers and give your car a good spin. They were also expert with buckets of water for getting rid of any vomit that may have been thrown up. Going on the waltzers with a bellyful of candyfloss, spuds and fizzy drinks was not really to be advised. The ghost train was another ride not to be missed. You paid your money and got into the little car, which was generally pulled by an engine that would be made up to look like an old-time Western cowboy railroad engine. The wagons would fill up with what looked like braver souls than you as you sat there with mounting trepidation. Then with a hoot of its horn you would slowly enter the tunnel through its swing-doors painted like a devil's mouth. Inside it was pitch black and the sounds of the engine would suddenly be drowned by the screams of the terrified kids. Things would touch you in the dark, skeleton hands would try to capture you, demonic faces would suddenly appear lit from underneath and looking like your worst nightmare. Sometimes there would be a fairground worker hidden in the gloom and he would grab your arms or legs or touch your face as you went past. Deafening screams were evident by this time, as a type of mass hysteria gripped the captured, fear-filled passengers. Was ever money so well spent? Then just as suddenly as you had gone into the pitch-black tunnel, you emerged back into the bright lights, eyes blinking, and trying to look unconcerned, and to be laughed at by the watching crowd if you were caught with your head buried in your arms or below the seat, as very many a so-called rough, tough Astonite lad was. Then the inevitable long walk home, dirty, tired, deaf, the winners carrying their doom-laden fish, and the plaster of Paris dogs that made great chalk for marking out hopscotch games when they finally got broken. Poor? Maybe, but some of the happiest kids in the world nevertheless.

In 1952 my school days in the Cowper Street Juniors were finished. They asked me which senior school I wanted to go to and I said Upper Thomas Street, which was where my mate was going to go. When I went home and told our mom she went mad at me. "I went to Summer Lane, my brothers and sisters went to Summer Lane and you are going to go to Summer Lane". So I rolled up on the first day of school, and because I was not on the books, I was put into class 1D. After about two weeks in this class I was sent up to 1A, the top class for that year. Summer Lane School was a whole new world, and a daunting place for a first-year pupil. Surrounded by much bigger boys and girls, you were once again a little fish in a very big pond. Some of the elder kids would smoke in the outside toilets although discipline was generally very tight. We were taught by what seemed to be mainly Welsh teachers, and very good they were too. These people from the hard-working mining village communities appeared to have an affinity with the hard-done-by kids of Aston. Not only were we taught the arts, but hands-on things too; carpentry being a favourite among most of the lads. The carpentry shop was on its own down the end of the schoolyard, and the teacher was a little bald-headed bloke. He taught us to the best of his ability, but woe betide any lad that made a mistake in his class. He would prowl around the workshop with a large wooden mallet clutched in his thick fingers, and creeping up on his unsuspecting victim, would suddenly smash this mallet onto the worktop with such a force that it made all the tools on it leap in the air, and at the same time shouted, "Gather round here boys!" When the class had collected around the poor boy's workbench, he would make him repeat the terrible wrong he had done in front of his classmates, who were only too pleased that it wasn't them standing there so isolated. Then he would lay into him verbally. Sometimes if you gave him any sort of lip he would give you a slap around the face with his thick chubby fingers for your cheek: no running home to mommy claiming assault; you were just glad he hadn't reported you to the headmaster, who would have dealt out six of the best.

The workshop had a loft where various woods were kept, and in our later years, a mate and me would creep up the stairs to have a crafty fag. I am sure that the pong of the glue, which smelled like a combination of boiled horses' hooves, bones and smelly feet, masked the cigarette smoke quite easily. It certainly was overpowering. One of the projects we tackled was a little triangular table. You could buy whatever you had made and this one cost five bob. Our mom had it in her house for years after. She wouldn't throw it away because it had cost so much.

Swimming lessons for us kids who went to Summer Lane School were at the Woodcock Street Baths, a wonderful old building on the edge of town. The lads' dressing rooms were full of little kids, playing each other up, flicking each others' arses with what they called their towels. These could be pieces of material made of almost anything, and could range in size from blanket to handkerchief proportions. The swimming trunks worn were weird and wonderful, to say the least — from multi-coloured ones made of scraps of curtain or frocks, to the dreaded woollen ones. These fine examples of woollen art made lovingly by some hard-working mom slaving in front of her tiny fireplace, for her poor little boy or girl, became absolute disasters when wet. The unfortunate kid who happened to own one of these nightmares would find that on entering the water, the costume would slowly become heavier and heavier, and stretch below their knees, while being held at the waist by a string belt. It would in some cases drop completely off the unsuspecting swimmer so that they would be larking about strip naked! Sometimes it was hard to retain what little dignity you had if you were showing your all to your sniggering classmates, while trying to rescue the heavy unwieldy garment from the bottom of the pool. There were kids that had swimming nicks and costumes that had been lovingly dyed to make them look like the real thing; again on land they would look great but when the dye slowly started to ooze out, the owner of this piece of clothing would be followed around the baths by a cloud of whatever colour the swimwear had been dyed in. The baths were in some cases the only time a kid would have a chance to meet water in large quantities, and there was many a little street urchin who stood under the shower desperately trying to clean himself with no soap, his skinny, blackened feet skidding on the tiles. The changing rooms were a place where no one could hide, and all your clothing was on full view to your peers: spuds in socks were a must, cardboard in shoe-bottoms, shirts that had been converted from ladies' blouses, no underpants, and hand-me-downs. There was no hiding place and all was revealed in this room. When you finally got into the chlorine-impregnated water it was best if you kept just your head above the water because of the cold, but it could sometimes be a problem trying to avoid the green snot that every kid seemed to be full of. Every shout and every word would echo up to the glass roof and back down in a sometimes-deafening roar. When you got out of the baths it was so cold that your teeth could literally rattle with your violent shivering. Pulling clothes onto wet, shivering bodies could be a really hard thing to accomplish, but as ever, we managed.

Swimming lessons over and feeling refreshed, a visit to the café was a must. This café sold mugs of chocolate for a penny a go. It was fantastic, sweet, hot and tasty; this mug of chocolate was worth all the previous embarrassments, panic and fears to taste. After being in the baths, as you walked home in the gloom, the street lights seemed to have halos around them. It must have been the chlorine and whatever other chemicals they put into the water that did it.

As well as the swimming baths, the school would send us to the playing fields down by Perry Common. Football was the favourite sport for the lads, and however poor you were, everyone seemed to own a pair of football boots. These boots were made of hard-as-iron leather, had steel toecaps, and could be lethal weapons on the feet of an inept player. I had a pair of hand-me-downs that had to be packed with paper to make them fit; I must have looked as if I had Charlie Chaplin boots on they were that big. To run in these hard, heavy, mud-laden boots took an almost

Herculean effort, so the game, especially when it was wet, would proceed at a leisurely pace, and if the ball stopped in a puddle you had a much better chance of injuring yourself if you tried kicking it out. If you got kicked in the shin or anywhere else for that matter by these blunt instruments of torture, you would be bruised for ages. To try to soften them up you would spend hours dubbing them; this meant rubbing them in dubbin, a greasy concoction, in a vain attempt to ease the leather. The ball was made of real leather, and when it was wet it used to weigh a ton. If you tried to head it and didn't get it right the ball would thud into your head like a wet sack of spuds, jarring your head and causing you to drop to your knees. To try to kick this bladder of lard any distance was almost impossible with the skinny legs most of the lads had, and anyone who could kick this thing properly was secretly admired. The only football strip we ever had consisted of a blue or red ribbon worn over your shoulder and down to your waist. But when you wore this strip you were supposed to support your fellow team-mates, whoever they were, and this was sometimes done with real gusto, especially if you had a bone to pick with an opposing player. There was many an old score settled on these playing fields. Tennis was also played with borrowed balls and rackets: no whites for us lot, and you couldn't half slide on the gravel in your borrowed school footwear.

Summer Lane School held dancing lessons for its elder pupils, which in some instances could be embarrassing for boys and girls of fourteen or so, especially if the teacher picked you out for doing something wrong. Some of the lads were dressed in shorts so tight that their arses looked like shiny billiard balls. Several of these dancers wore hob-nailed boots, some turned-down wellingtons and some, like me, second-hand shoes. The noise made on the wooden floor by this exotic footwear was deafening and used to resound off the ceiling.

Gymnastics was taught at school as well. The lads would have to strip to the waist, their skinny ribs showing like the rabbits we used to have. Shorts were no problem because most lads wore them as normal attire. Footwear was a pair of pumps supplied from a locked pigeon-hole cage. I suppose this was to stop them being nicked. I got to love gymnastics and was quite good at it, so much so that when I was about fourteen, my mate and I were picked to represent Birmingham at the BAI centre in Birmingham. I stuck it for about six months and although I was good enough to have been part of the squad, I eventually couldn't stand the embarrassment of not having the proper shorts, underpants, pumps and vest, and never owning a proper towel or being able to go for a shower with the other lads on the team who were mostly grammar school boys, and who had proper towels, a change of clothes, and real sports bags to carry it all in. I never told my mom the reason that I had left; I just said I wasn't good enough.

CHAPTER
FOUR

Good Times,
Bad Times

The year 1953 was one to remember; the Coronation was due in June and everyone in Cowper Street had been saving a tanner a week for months to have a good time on the big day. Because we lived on the corner of Cowper Street and Summer Lane, no one seemed to have asked our house to put into the kitty. As a consequence, I was not invited to the sit-down street party that was put on. But whoever (bless them) organised this event did allow me to join in all the races and games that went on after the party, so that I wasn't made to feel a complete outsider. The trimmings went right across the yards and street; Union Jack flags were everywhere. Lots of the women wore red, white and blue clothes and some of the men had on flag-coloured boaters. The food was laid out on tables in abundance and for people and kids that had suffered years of penny-pinching rationing, it was a sight to be seen. There were races and games all day, the winners receiving a Coronation medal. None came my way, but I felt I was welcomed into the fold by these good-hearted Brummies. That night a lot of the blokes went round to the bombed peck on the corner of Ormond Street and Summer Lane opposite the Birmingham Arms and proceeded to rip down the hoardings that were on the corner. These made a great bonfire and much beer was imbibed around it, with roast spuds aplenty, and the hole it burned into the middle of the street was there for ages. A mute reminder of something to celebrate for once.

In our house the coronation was one of the last few nice things to happen for a long time to come. At the beginning of 1953, after thirty years' hard work in front of glass-blowing furnaces my dad and his brother were given one week's notice and fired. He received no compensation, and with five kids to feed, this was really tough. Luckily our mom had a job at the time and was able to provide food for us all. Our dad, who had no other trade than glass-blower, was given a job on a building site by the local unemployment office, and he became a brickie's labourer. This was a disastrous move, because within weeks he had fallen down a ladder from just three feet, and had broken both legs. It was judged by the doctors that the years he had spent in front of the furnaces had made his bones brittle. He spent months with both legs in plaster, and because where we lived was above a chemist's shop, if he went out he had to lower himself step by step down a steep flight of stairs and when he got back then had to drag himself backwards up them to get into the house. He had a wheelchair and I would sometimes push him over the road to the Three Horse Shoes, where he would have a couple of pints with his mates. In August 1953, at the age of forty-five, our dad had obviously had enough of being in plaster, and of having no job prospects. The strain of not working and not pulling his weight must have been enormous, and at two in the morning one August day, he mixed a cup of water and arsenic (which he had used in his glass-blowing days), drank it, struggled up to the attic and threw himself out of the window head first.

The coroner's verdict was suicide while the balance of his mind was disturbed. Whose mind wouldn't have been disturbed with what he had gone through? There was a small write-up in the local paper, and that seemed to me to be the total sum of this man's life. The final ignominy was that they wouldn't allow his coffin into the church at his burial. I wasn't allowed to go to the funeral because suicides were considered unfit for a Christian send-off, and I suppose our mom didn't want me to see what happened. The scars of his ill-treatment by people in power, by getting rid of him from work out of hand like a worn-out animal, the lack of compassion from the church (the one place you would expect understanding from), deeply affected me and remains with me still. After our dad's death his brother lost all heart to live and he too soon passed away. Mom's brother also succumbed to TB and died that year and our grandad a year later. This meant that four of our mom's closest relatives had died within a year.

If we hadn't been desperate before, we were now. Our mom now had two kids at school, one girl at work on two pounds a week, one lad at technical school, and another son in the Army. Because of our situation, us two younger kids were given free school dinner tickets. These free tickets were a different colour than the ones that other paying kids had, so when it came to putting food on your plate the servers all knew who was who, and some of them served accordingly. On the eight-seater table I sat at there was no one who had both parents alive: a real sign of the times. Limp lettuce, soggy tomatoes, a bit of onion, crinkly, curled-at-the-edges bread and spam acted the part of a salad; lumpy potato mash (two scoops and that's your lot), greasy, thick, brown gravy, things that hid under the gravy called vegetables, gristly fatty meats, runny rice puddings, rhubarb that made your face pucker like you were sucking a lemon, covered with either a thin watery custard or a thick gluey custard with its thick skin on top, were all wolfed down. These dinners were usually the main meal of the day for some of these kids. Despite its content, if you collected all the plates and took them to the counter you could sometimes get an extra pudding, so there was never any shortage of hungry kids taking plates back.

Through all these hardships our mom would never let me have *Daily Mail* boots, or socks: I think she considered that these things were only for the really poor. At this time I was wearing a pair of "Sally Anne's" big, brown leather brogues, not really the sort of footwear that was common in Cowper Street, and nailed into the heels with brass tacks were the initials of the rich kid who had given them to the poor. These initials had cost me a punch-up when some kid wanted to know what the initials meant. Obviously I had no answer, so fisticuffs ensued. The *Daily Mail* hob-nailed horrors had three holes punched into the leather so that kids in the know knew what you had on and would let everyone else know too.

Because I was impressed with the marching and band-playing that went on, I decided to join the Boys' Brigade. The meetings of the branch I went to were held at a church on Sixways, Aston. We had to go to the church on Sundays to sing in the choir and pass the collection plates along the aisles. I, like most of the cherubic kids of Aston, became adept at flicking the bottom of the collection plate so it sounded as if you had put money into it, and taking a tanner or a bob out for change; this made all the choir-singing worthwhile. The long-suffering bloke who ran the brigade was the local truant officer for the Aston area. As I was very good at gymnastics, he was keen to keep me in the brigade, but after a couple of months I stopped going. The next time I saw him he asked me why I hadn't been to the meetings. I said the only thing that came into my head: that I hadn't got any proper footwear. Imagine the horror of it all when a week later he presented me in front of our whole class, not only a pair of boots, but thick grey socks and a pair of pumps as well. Our mom was absolutely mortified, and needless to say I never wore any of them. "We are not that poor yet", she would say.

CHAPTER
FIVE

Happy Campers

When we had moved to Summer Lane, my eldest sister knew a girl who lived just down the lane by Milton Street. She had five or six brothers and they lived in the back part of a house up an entry, the front being bomb-damaged, I think. I used to go with my sister to their house and made friends with the youngest lad. The family, whose parents were both dead, had no one to look after them and the eldest sister was their surrogate mom. When she got married and left, the younger sister took over the mantle of mother. This family had an old bell tent at a place called Holte Fleet, and because I was now a mate, I was invited to join them on a camping holiday. Our mom somehow found the five bob that was going to keep me going for the next two weeks and, carrying all my possessions, including tins of beans and a loaf of bread in an old kit bag, off we went. We got off the Midland Red bus at a place called Ombersley, and walked down country lanes until we reached a farm where the tent was stored in an old barn. This tent was an old green and brown camouflaged Army one which weighed a ton, but willing hands had soon erected it. It was cold, wet and draughty, the roof leaked when it rained and if you touched the sides, the rain would come through at that point. It didn't matter a bit; it was our place and we loved it. The inevitable rain pattering on the tent when you were trying to get to sleep had a wonderful effect on you, lying there warm as toast, the gentle noise would send you off in no time, and it was all the better for being free. You also had to be careful where you put the tent, otherwise you would find streams of water running through it at night. But whatever else it was, it was our home for two weeks, a palace in the countryside for kids who generally lived their lives in cramped, mean streets with no grass, no trees and fog and smoke the norm. We seemed to live for two whole weeks on tins of beans, and knocked-off eggs all cooked in the black frying pan that was stored with the tent. The flatulent results of this desperate diet were at once both hilarious and serious. Hilarious because of the many different trumpet sounds and smells of farts that would rebound off the walls of the tent, and serious because if you were caught short it was the nearest ditch and you'd better be quick.

Our beds were straw and grass under an old tarpaulin, and your clothes and whatever you could get hold of were your blankets. The freedom from adults and school was great. To come from the run-down, closed-in back terraced houses of Aston, and to be let free to do what you wanted, where the horizon was not smoking factory chimney stacks, and thumping noises, but real trees and green grass, could not be bettered. After living with the sounds of the Lucas night shift at

Hockley invading our bedroom all the time, to have almost complete silence was most unnerving, but you soon got used to it. I had never seen real live cows, sheep or pigs before and was fascinated by them, and found it hard to link them to the food that you ate, not that we had much chance of eating fresh meat. The river was where we washed, the camping site then being just a field, with no toilets, no washrooms, and no interference. We played all day below the weir in the River Severn, and sometimes for a penny we would get a ride on the river with legs straddling the sides of a rubber dinghy, a business that some enterprising Black Country bloke had set up; "river trips a penny", read the sign, sailing into the sunset on a pirate ship in the mind. We watched the swallows build their nests under the bridge that spanned the river, and we bird-nested with impunity. There was a riverside pub down the banks called The Wharf where kids even as young as us could get into, a little insight into the world of beer-drinkers that was not normally allowed. It reeked of cigarette smoke and the smell of beer. I met a girl in the campsite one day and took a liking to her. When I asked her where she came from she said, "Tiptun". Hoping to impress this girl from a strange exotic sounding place with my Tarzan-type antics, I climbed a tree and I when I got to the top promptly slipped while trying to hang upside down and came crashing down into the stream below, knocking myself out for a few minutes. When I came to my new friend had vanished, leaving me with cuts and bruises and splinters, and a battered ego. Whenever I saw her with her friends after that she would talk behind her hands to them and they would all laugh looking my way as they walked off. These camping trips are now treasured memories of a time that will never return, and we are all the poorer because of it.

When I had made friends with a few more people at Summer Lane School, I was invited to go camping with a load of lads from New John Street West. These intrepid travellers went further afield than my first trips and they would go as far as Tewkesbury.

The campsite was not far from the cathedral, and had a small stream running through it. This stream was host to a variety of living things, such as moorhens, frogs, small fish and when the time of the year was right, millions of elvers. We would get out of the tent late at night and go to the little weir on the stream, and there in the moonlight would be thousands of the small elvers trying to get up the weir. It really was a sight to remember. There were people around who would catch and eat these tiny eels but it never appealed to us. The New John Street mob were adventurous souls and we would range far and wide around Tewkesbury and the surrounding countryside. One year we all bought little axes from the Woolworth's shop in Tewkesbury and spent hours like the Redskins in the cowboy movies, throwing these weapons at trees trying to make them stick into the wood. On our travels we had come across a piggery that had dozens of piglets running free in a field; we would feed these little porkers on the crab apples we got from the trees in the lane. We would line up along the fence and all shout "Oy, oy, oy!" and these little piglets would race out of their pens like the Charge of the Light Brigade. Great fun to watch, this harmless bit of fun only stopped when we were caught by the farmer one day and he gave the biggest lad a slap around the face, telling us to go away in no uncertain terms. Night-time held no fear for these lads and we would go for long walks up the riverbanks, and once we ran about five miles back to the campsite under a full moon, with moonbeams lighting up the river like a silver road. Two weeks of this relaxing holiday and we came home shattered but happy. Once when there were just two of us camping it rained for days on end and our tiny two-man tent was saturated and in danger of being washed away. We were on the verge of having to go home when a couple of fishermen camping nearby offered to help us. This offer turned out to be all four of us going to the docks at midnight and stealing a large tarpaulin off a boat that was moored there. This tarpaulin was big enough to go under our tent and back over the top; the heroes helped to move us to higher ground and our holiday was saved. These two Good Samaritans were in Tewkesbury for the night eel-fishing and would let us go with them as long as we kept quiet. Sitting up all night with the rain beating down on the big umbrellas we sat under, and waiting for the whirr of the ratchet on the fishing reels, was every little lad's dream come true. These men fishing by the weir would use the bleak they had caught during the day as bait: they stank to high heaven, but it worked as they caught some really big eels. One of them was three feet long!

As the dawn neared and the coal-black night began to recede, the river would get lighter and there would sometimes be a river mist hovering about two or three feet above the water. If you got down low enough you could see the other bank beneath. As it got lighter, slowly the sky changed from black to silver, to pink and the sun, when it came out, burned off the mist to reveal two tired, hungry, fish-bait-smelling happy kids.

Wintertime had its own problems, getting coal, trying to keep warm, the snot freezing along your sleeves where you had wiped your nose, the insides of the house windows freezing up and Jack Frost painting his whirling frozen pictures for you to admire. When you breathed on the windows you could thaw out little round holes to see out of. Warm clothes were at a premium, and for instance, I was just fourteen before I got my first pair of long trousers. It was nice to have some sort of cover for my battle hardened, scarred blue knees. I can't remember where these trousers came from but they made me feel grown-up wearing them. In the school playground we lads would make huge icy slides, and as a sign of courage, you had to run at them full pelt and go flying down these "slopes of death", arms and coats all over the place and, if you slipped and fell, you were jeered all the way to the bottom by your peers. The slides were packed on both sides by mobs of kids; as you flew past them their faces were just a blur, and because of this there was many a lad tripped up as he flew down the icy track, and injuries were not uncommon. Snowball fights were also a must and sometimes the schoolyard would resemble a blizzard with snowballs replacing snowflakes. The on-duty playground teachers, who had no chance of stopping this storm of flying hard-as-ice missiles, would retreat to the toilet block for a fag until the storm abated. If you scraged or cut yourself the school would send you to the school clinic; the one we used to go to was up by Six Ways, Aston. At the junction you could stand for ages watching the copper who stood in the middle of the road directing the traffic like some musical conductor. They were great at it and fascinating to watch, and no one dared to go out of turn. If you walked at the right pace you could take a couple of hours to get there and back, and the nurses would tend to your wounds with tut-tutting care. Whatever the injury was, the cure always seemed to be the same: paint the injured part blue, and bandage it with a pristine white bandage. These blue-and-white repair jobs would be like badges of courage to us kids and we wore them with pride; anything to make you stand out from the crowd was a bonus.

CHAPTER
SIX

Making a Bob or Two

It goes without saying that money was at a premium and it taxed our brains how to get our hands on any at all. Milk and pop bottles all had a penny deposit put on them, so we would always be on the lookout for them. There was one small shop, run by an old couple, on the corner of Ormond Street and Newtown Row, that sold both milk and pop. Unfortunately, they used to keep the returned pop and milk bottles in a fenced-off area up the backyard. We had no real problem at all with getting over this fence and taking a few bottles at a time; these would be taken round to the shop and the penny refund duly paid. I don't think the old man ever cottoned on to what was happening, and all I can say in my defence is "desperate times breed desperate measures". You could get a halfpenny and put silver paper on it and if you rubbed it in your hair the king's head would come through; to take this fake bob into a shop took some guts but if you got away with it the rewards were nice. There was a small shop down the lane that would pay a shilling a pound for real wool. I stole a kid's jumper one day and spent hours and hours unravelling the thing. Taking the rolled-up wool to the shop, I was already spending my ill-gotten gains, and was most severely disappointed when the shopkeeper said that it wasn't real wool. Twisters never prosper. Me and my mate would steal white mice to order. This was quite easy: we just went to town to the Bull Ring and at the top was a pet shop called Pimms. After spending ages trying to get the big parrot they had at the front of the shop to swear, all you had to do was put your hands in the mouse box and let them run up your coat sleeve. Simple but effective. Standing in the coal queue in Cowper Street for three pence was another money-making venture, although it was no fun at all standing in the cold and rain being shouted at by the bloke who ran the coal yard. One day I had stood for ages to get a half-hundredweight of coal for a lady who lived down the street. There was no way I could afford the barrow and I was dragging this dead weight down the street when our mom, who must have seen me, came and gave me a hand. She practically carried this soggy, dirty, heavy-as-lead load to the woman's door for me, and when I got home she told me never to do it again, as it was like begging. On a Monday our mom would take me with her down to the "pop shop". This was a place in Newtown Row that had three brass balls hanging outside of it and you went up a yard and through a door and there behind a wire-enclosed counter sat the man who was going to supply you with enough money to live for a week, in exchange for your dad's best mainly threadbare suit. One and three pence he would offer, "make it one and nine pence, please", mom would say, and before long, to the mutual satisfaction of both parties, the princely sum of one and sixpence would be arrived at. See you Friday? he would ask. No, it will be Saturday, was the reply.

Around Christmas time was always good for earning money by carol-singing. Me and a mate went to most of the pubs in the lane, opened the latch door and sang, standing just inside the smoke-filled bars and lounges. There were times when the landlord would try to throw us out but an angry muttering of his clientele would soon put a stop to it. For three nights on the trot we earned the magnificent sum of thirty bob each: it was like being a millionaire. It came to an end though when we tried to go round the same pubs for the third time: "Sod off you little bleeders", was the reaction this time. There were all sorts of blokes plying their trade around the pubs; from mouth organ players to the ones who would play the accordions; from periwinkles to stuff that had fallen off a lorry, you could get the lot around the pubs in Aston. As I got older and the back-to-backs started to be emptied by the council, me and a mate would break into the vacated tenements to steal the money out of the gas meters. They only had a tiny brass lock on them, and I don't suppose they thought anyone would ever break into them, so it was easy pickings for us.

This sort of venture led to me and a couple of mates breaking into the chemist's shop that I lived over. It was so easy to do. We broke the small window over the back door and just undid the bolt. This burglary was so exciting to us that we were nearly pissing ourselves with fear and delight: fear that if we were caught we would be put away in the approved school for at least three years, and delight because we had found the key to the cash drawer in the pocket of a white coat that was hanging on the door. When we opened the drawer there before us lay about a hundred and fifty quid in cash. An absolute fortune. The cops from Bridge Street police station came down but they never even spoke to me, although I had got the stub of a cinema ticket from the Newtown Row picture house to prove where I had been. My mom would have absolutely killed me if she had found out; bringing shame on the family was a thing you never did. Me and my mate finally used some of these ill-gotten gains to put deposits down on bikes at the bike shop on Six Ways. These bikes were called Dawes' Double Blue, and would transport us from the mean streets of Aston to the rolling fields and countryside of Worcester and beyond.

To cover my being able to pay off the HP, I got a part-time job at a little shop that sold wood and DIY stuff. This shop was next to the factory that made funeral shrouds on the opposite side of the road to the Globe and on the hill to Six Ways. My hours were four to six every night and eight to one on Saturdays. I had to run there from school during the week so as not to be late. My duties included sweeping up the back room where the wood-working machines were, putting all the bundles of wood back into the store area from outside where they were displayed for sale, and sometimes using the planing machine to flatten wood. I eventually left this little job and suggested to the owner that he employ a mate of mine instead. When I next saw my mate he was as happy as Larry. It turned out he was selling the wood bundles from the front of the shop and pocketing the cash; he had tripled his money and had built up his own clientele who would only go to him to be served. Enterprising, to say the least. When I left the wood shop I got another job with a local bloke who had a tiny workshop off the back of Lozells Road. He made wooden spade handles, and this time I got to work the machines as well as carrying out my cleaning jobs.

When we were both fourteen, me and my mate got work with his brother who was a roof tiler by trade. This is where the bikes came in handy as the work he did was mostly over towards Lichfield, Burton-upon-Trent, and that sort of area. We would ride our bikes from Aston, down the A38, through Sutton Coldfield and beyond. Some of these journeys would be as much as twenty-five miles. When we got to wherever the house to be tiled was, our job was to load the roof. This meant carrying the tiles on your shoulder up a two-storey ladder to the roof, then onto the roof lathes and put them where required. We would count these trips as a matter of pride and one hundred journeys loaded down with concrete tiles was not to be sniffed at. We were offered the bus and train fare but preferred to ride to the sites — the fare money coming in handy for other things. Looking back, it seems amazing that two skinny little kids could ride for as much as up to twenty-five miles, spend all day carrying heavy tiles onto a two-storey roof, and then ride back again. If we weren't working for a weekend we would ride off into the countryside and if we found a building site we would find the key to the builder's shed (generally under a brick by the shed door), and take the key to the dumper machine. We could spend hours driving this thing around the sites. One freezing winter's day, when it was too icy to ride our bikes, we took the train out to the newly built Butlers Lane railway station. Walking towards the building site, the ice crackling in the frozen little puddles we trod in, the trees were covered in ice a quarter of an inch thick, shining like hard diamonds. Cobwebs hanging in the hedges looked like the most delicate pieces of jewelled lace, the sun shining through the ice on them giving them wonderful colours. A crisp, hard day where the air was so cold and fresh it took your breath away and replaced it with the joys of life. Then to work up and down an icy ladder onto a roof full of slippery, icy perils. The roof tiles, when they were wet and gritty, would eventually wear the skin off your fingertips, but this wasn't too bad unless they bled; then they became painful, the cement in the tiles burning your raw fingers. Sometimes you would grab a nail from your nail pouch and the sharp end would dig into the hole in your finger — this certainly kept you awake. These trips were great because they got you out into the countryside; they gave you a taste of what work was going to be like, and most importantly of all, you got paid for it.

CHAPTER
SEVEN

A Bit of a Laugh

Of course life wasn't all doom and gloom, all work and graft and nicking things — there was lots of fun to be had around the lane and its locality. For instance, down by Asylum Road there was a little joke shop which sold all sorts of items: masks, jumping beans and magic tricks. It also sold fantastic stink bombs. These little glass phials held all of the world's worst smells: rotten eggs smelled like perfume compared to these little horrors. While we were flush with our illicitly gained wealth, me and my mate would buy some of these glass bombs, wait by the bus stop in Summer Lane just by Cowper Street, and when the bus came along and stopped for us, we would get on and throw the bombs down the bus and immediately leap off the platform. It was a delight to hear people shouting and moaning about the stink as the bus sailed off towards town, its captive travellers trapped in a sulphurous cloud of stench. The Three Horse Shoes also came in for its fair whack of bombs: a quick open of the latch door, a throw into the bar, then hang onto the door handle with all your might, laughing like drains as the unfortunate recipients got the full brunt of the phials' contents. Of course you had to brave and very, very quick on your feet to play this game.

Going up the Monkey Run was a cheap form of entertainment. Our walk would take us down Cowper Street, left into Newtown Row looking in the shop windows as we went along, up past the Globe and the Aston Hip to Six Ways, then a turn left onto Lozells Road (again window shopping, talking and dreaming of a future yet to be decided) as we went along Villa Road onto Soho Hill, down the hill to Hockley Brook, left into Farm Street and in no time, an hour and half or so had vanished, the world had been put to rights, you had sorted out the way you wanted your world to be to you, you were happy and tired, and things didn't seem so bad after all.

Another prank of ours was to get hold of an old purse or handbag, tie fishing line to it, and place it on the pavement. When our victim tried to pick it up, we would yank it away: this certainly made people jump. A bob stuck to the pavement was just as funny; fingernails could be cracked trying to retrieve this bit of silver. Three times a week me and my mate would walk up to Park Lane to catch the number eight bus to the Waldorf roller skating rink. You could hire skates for a bob a time, and for this price you would get anything the attendant threw at you. Sometimes your feet would be pulled in opposite directions to where you wanted them to go, with the occasional cross-legged accident occurring. If, on the other hand, you gave the bloke a tanner on top you would be handed a new(ish) pair of skates. Kitted out with these skates, we would go flying round the rink, trying to impress the girls who would slowly rotate around the outside, nattering to each other and seemingly oblivious to what the boys were getting up to. Trying to chat one of these girls up could be an absolute nightmare. You had to skate past her mates being scrutinised all the while by black mascara-eyed girls, and if, as was mostly the case, they laughed at you, it could be an acutely embarrassing experience, to say the least. Suddenly from nowhere a chain would evolve; there would be as many as fifty kids all hanging onto each other for grim life flying around the rink at a death-defying pace. The attendants would try to stop this suicidal crocodile of kids but they had no chance. When you joined this mad train you always hoped that there would be someone behind you because if you were last you were in great danger of being thrown off the chain and sent flying through the air at breakneck speed, sometimes with disastrous results. Broken legs and arms were the norm. Still, as long as it wasn't you, it didn't matter.

A favourite place when we got a bit older was the market opposite Lewis's. It had fruit and veg, curtain shops, leather goods, and the main attraction for us kids was an amusement arcade at the back. A pinball machine, test your strength, bingo; it had the lot. One day they installed a new-fangled talking machine. This was situated in a box like a telephone booth and you would put your tanner in and speak into the mike, and then listen back to the recording of what you had said. Hearing your own voice was hilarious and obviously being kids, the air would be really ripe, to say the least.

One day me and my mate were both jammed in this box when a teddy boy walked into the market. He had on a red coat with a black velvet collar, blue drainpipe trousers, brown suede winkle-pickers and slicked-back black hair done with a Bill Haley-style question mark. He was the genuine article, and he knew it. We immediately started taking the mickey out of him; tearing his clothes and looks to bits as he swaggered up towards us. Then, horror of horrors, he opened the booth door just as the tape machine played back our unflattering comments. We were terror-stricken but luckily for us, he was oblivious to the fact that it was him who we were ridiculing, saying what a great invention the tape machine was. A fast retreat was promptly executed before he cottoned on.

The pictures was always a favourite pastime and whole families would go to the local flicks together, some of them carrying bowls of soup for the old man who had just got there straight from work. Aston had a lot of picture houses. There was the Newtown Row, the Globe, with its wooden benches — the cheapest cinema seats in Brum, the Orient at Six Ways, and the Odeon on the Birchfield Road. The queues to these houses of entertainment could be quite long and so each cinema would have an usher to control the crowd. He would be a bloke dressed in an Army-type uniform with lots of gold braid and a peaked cap. Most of these blokes must have been ex-Army types because they were always shouting at you and pushing people back into line. The exception was the Globe where you paid four pence to sit at the front on the benches with a fancy red rope dividing you from the richer clientele behind you who paid a tanner to sit on real seats. There was no upstairs to this place. If you and your mate sat either side of the rope you would hear the patter of feet as kids ran down the aisle to go to the toilets; then they would jump over the rope and if you were quick enough you could whip it up and catch them in full flight. Of course if the kid you caught was bigger than you, you scarpered away pretty smartly. The Orient up Six Ways was a bit of a posh picture house where you could roll up at the pictures after the films had started and wait for people to come out who had seen all the programmes. You waited outside, and when seats were available the usher would say two, three or four please; you then went in and found your seats with the help of the torch-bearing usherette. One night when I was on a first date with a girl I decided to impress her by taking her to the Orient. We got there and waited in the queue for half an hour or so until the usher said there were two seats available and in we went. After standing outside in the glaring lights of the foyer, to go inside was to enter what resembled a coal pit of darkness, with the only light coming from the screen and the small wall lights. Standing there with a protective arm around my new date, I saw the two empty seats at the end of the back row, and there being no usherette in sight, I whispered to my date that I had spotted the seats. We struggled all the way down the line of patient patrons, with them having to stand up and let us pass. Things dropped on the floor and there was a general sense of being tut-tutted all the way along. I got to the two end seats and promptly sat down on a bloke's lap, my girl almost sitting on his female partner's lap. Against the wall these people, both wearing dark clothes, were almost invisible in the darkness. This incident had two immediate effects on me, one was that the girl vanished, and two, I found that I needed specs.

When it came close to you leaving school, you got an interview with the school careers officer. This man was supposed to look at your school record and listen to you and then try to find you a job that suited you. After all, this was possibly going to be be the job you would do for the rest of your life. I told him I wanted to work on a farm, and far from listening to me, he pooh-poohed the idea. "You don't want to get up at four in the morning in the snow and rain, milking cows and mucking out the pigs. No my lad, an engineering job is what you want", and because of his encouragement, dedication and commitment to his finding the employment I never wanted, I found myself one Monday morning as factory fodder reporting to the charge-hand in the engineering shop at the Norton motorbike factory in Bracebridge Street. Our mom had got me a new pair of bib-and-brace overalls to start my new job in, and one of the first things I did when I got the chance was to rub suds, oil and grease down the legs and across the front so I looked like a real worker. My time as a toolmaker was to be a short-lived career: no one seemed to have time to tell me what to do. I suppose the blokes were on piecework and money was their first priority. Whatever the reason, I was shown how to line up the cutting tool bit against the face of the leather belt-driven lathe so that it was square to the work. One day, having done this setting up, I was really pleased with myself; I felt grown up and thought I was beginning to fit in as a toolmaker. Unfortunately, I had forgotten to back off the cutting bit from the lathe face and when I pulled the overhead lever to set the lathe going, there was an almighty bang and the leather strap snapped in half. Back down to earth. I must have been a real nuisance to the charge-hand and hard-working blokes; all they wanted to do was make money and not have to keep showing a kid what to do. I would sit with my feet up on my lathe and throw small pieces of "swarf" into my suds oil can about ten feet away. I became really good at this and when I joined a darts team years later, this training stood me in good stead.

One day the long-suffering charge-hand sent me down to the stores with a four inch diameter length of steel, saying, "tell the bloke on the saw I want four pieces, three inches long, cut VF". I went down to the stores and when I told him the request the store man smiled and nodded to a stool, telling me to sit there and wait. It took him two days to cut these bits of steel, everything that had to be cut for others taking precedence. I finally asked him what VF meant, and he just laughed and said it meant "very fine". I was smoking at that time, as everybody did, and would sometimes run out of fags. No chance for nipping down the shop for a packet, so it would be down to the toilets to do my dad's old trick of picking up and smoking fag ends. Some had been flattened by dirty, oily boots, but when needs must . . .

You had to clock in and out of the factory and if you were three minutes late, it was as if you had committed a cardinal sin. You were up before the foreman and read the riot act. When we knocked off at lunchtime or at night, everybody would stand in the factory gateway waiting for the bell to go, then there would be an almighty rush to get onto the buses or whatever means of transport you had. I never waited and would get on my trusty Dawes's Double Blue and be gone as soon as I hit the gate. I lasted six weeks at this job. Being inside was torture to me, hanging around waiting to be given things to do by blokes who weren't interested was not my thing. The sun shining outside drew me like a moth to a lamp, and on top of that I couldn't stand the smell of the suds, oil, grease and red-hot "swarf".

I gave in my notice and got a job as a plumber's mate at a builder's yard in Heathfield Road, Handsworth. Within a couple of days I knew the building game was for me — going to different job sites, working outside in the summer, freezing your conkers off in the winter, meeting new blokes on every site, the laughs, the jokes, the singing that went on — to me it was magic. A whole new world opened up, and whereas before I had been a big fish in a little pond, the reverse was now true and I soon found out that taking the mickey out of these rough, tough building workers would get me a belt around the ear, or worse, a kick up the arse. "Not at school now, Sonny", they would say. These guys were craggy construction workers; most of them had fought in the Second World War, but as hard as they were, deep down they were mostly good-hearted Brummies. They also had to be patient men to put up with all the questions I used to throw at them: "What's this?" and "What's that for?" I was forever asking them. As far as I was concerned the chippies on the the job were golden. I don't think I ever saw a carpenter lose his rag, whatever the circumstances. They would be kneeling down fitting the locks or hinges to doors and would have to get up off their knees for anyone who had to go through the doorway, in some cases a dozen times or more.

It was the brickies, though, as far as I could see, who had it harder than anyone else on the building sites. They were literally expected to work outside regardless of the weather, manhandling the heavy bricks, concrete and cement. It cannot have been an easy life for them, but these blokes seemed happy enough. Us younger ones would try to impress each other with feats of strength like picking up so many bricks with one hand or trying to carry a bag of cement across the floor; the older blokes would be looking on until somebody had had enough and with casual ease would carry two bags of cement around, just to show us up.

We had enough weight training by having to carry sheets of lead up six or seven floors — no lifts back then — so everything had to be moved by our own brute force.

The very first big site I worked on was the new Marks & Spencer's, which was being built in town. We had to roll out large sheets of lead and the plumber would shape it to go under the window sills. The drainpipes were cast-iron and were jointed with molten lead, and it was my job to go to the room below wherever the lead was to be poured to make sure no-one was there, or anything else that could get burned, for that matter. One day, the lead went straight through to the floor below me and stuck to a load of coats hanging up there.

I learned there and then that you simply cannot get molten lead out of material.

All day long all you could hear was the bang of the weights that slammed onto the girders, hammering them into the soil that was going to be the new city of Birmingham. It was great working in Brum; you could have a walk around the old Rag Market or the Bull Ring and up and down the streets full of shops: those that were left, anyway. The difference between the freedom of working outside and working in a factory could not be compared. One day I had a run-in with the owner of the company. I had raced up to the top floor but I was five minutes late and he was standing there with his bowler hat on and his black overcoat unbuttoned, showing his waistcoat with its gold chain, and his large pocket watch in his hand.

"You are late!" he thundered, "and you are embezzling me out of money, fiddling your time sheet and taking money by false pretences."

When I pointed out that I hadn't done my time sheet yet, he just stood there gob-smacked. I don't suppose anyone had ever stood up to him and had the guts to point out the weakness in his argument. He just blustered on muttering about things like "in my day, blah, blah, blah."

This lesson of knowing my rights and being able to stand up to the bullies would stay with me all my working life. Can anyone tell me what was gained by driving all the way to town, climbing seven storeys of a building site, standing and waiting there to catch a kid who was working for the princely sum of a bob an hour and was five minutes late? How times change.

Acknowledgements

I would like to thank all the people who contributed to this book in one way or another, some through the generous loan of photographs, some through sharing their memories. My wife Sheila, who was also brought up in a back-to-back house in Cowper Street, Aston, has been a great help to me, as she always is. She has reminded me of lots of incidents and things that happened in our past lives together, filling in the blanks here and there when my memory wasn't so clear. I have had encouragement from my family and friends, both in the passing over of photographs and of the jogging of long-lost memories.

My brother Harry and sister Valerie have provided both photographs and reminders of our family life and have been very helpful regarding the past. They are as much a part of this book as I am.

In the last three years, my brother, sister and myself found two of our long-lost cousins: Derek Twist, who is the son of my dad's brother, Albert, and June Christie, the daughter of my dad's only sister, Dinah. These two cousins of ours managed to provide both photographs and memories of our family's past and for this I am very grateful. I want to thank my brother-in-law, Leo Bunting, for providing some of the photographs of Cowper Street, my other brother-in-law, John Gibbons and his wife Mary for encouragement and for other photographs and memories of Cowper Street.

Beryl Evans from The Old Summer Laners' Society, who is a mine of information, reminded me of things that happened at Summer Lane School many years ago.

I thank Michelle Tilling of The History Press for her help and positive attitude in making the publication of this book possible.

And last, but certainly not least, Professor Carl Chinn MBE, who supplied me not only with photos of Aston and Nechells, courtesy of Birmingham Lives (the Carl Chinn Archive) but with advice and encouragement. It was his suggestion that I try to get this book published that pushed me towards doing so. He has helped me, a complete stranger to him, by writing a foreword, and giving me some of his most precious time and advice. He really is a true Brummie.

My sincere thanks to all the above, and to all the people of Birmingham for being who you are.

ISIS publish a wide range of books in large print, from fiction to biography. Any suggestions for books you would like to see in large print or audio are always welcome. Please send to the Editorial Department at:

ISIS Publishing Limited
7 Centremead
Osney Mead
Oxford OX2 0ES

A full list of titles is available free of charge from:

Ulverscroft Large Print Books Limited

(UK)
The Green
Bradgate Road, Anstey
Leicester LE7 7FU
Tel: (0116) 236 4325

(Australia)
P.O. Box 314
St Leonards
NSW 1590
Tel: (02) 9436 2622

(USA)
P.O. Box 1230
West Seneca
N.Y. 14224-1230
Tel: (716) 674 4270

(Canada)
P.O. Box 80038
Burlington
Ontario L7L 6B1
Tel: (905) 637 8734

(New Zealand)
P.O. Box 456
Feilding
Tel: (06) 323 6828

Details of **ISIS** complete and unabridged audio books are also available from these offices. Alternatively, contact your local library for details of their collection of **ISIS** large print and unabridged audio books.

One O' Them Girls in Blue

Pat Lacey

"I was rather proud of having been referred to as 'one o' them girls in blue' I smiled to myself, filing it away in my mind to tell my mother about when next I wrote."

Pat Lacey grew up in Abergavenny in the years leading up to the Second World War. Her first job was as a telegraphist and the desire to sign up when war broke out eventually saw her assigned to the WAAF as a teleprinter at RAF Benson. Taking her trusty bike "George" with her she made many friends, learning to dance and stepping out with boys. Pat was at her post as D-Day happened and heard the news from her roommate, a wireless operator.

Pat shares her war years, the loss of her older brother, her first taste of alcohol and even her first holiday abroad in this warm hearted memoir.

ISBN 978-0-7531-9546-8 (hb)
ISBN 978-0-7531-9547-5 (pb)